Praise for Andrea McLean

'I greatly admire how Andrea fearlessly shares her recovery journey in the pursuit of serving others. Let her story inspire you to transform and grow.'
GABRIELLE BERNSTEIN, #1 NEW YORK TIMES BESTSELLING AUTHOR OF THE UNIVERSE HAS YOUR BACK

'Andrea is a glorious human being and an inspiring writer - she is going to help so many people with this wonderful, healing book.'
BRYONY GORDON, #1 BESTSELLING AUTHOR AND AWARD-WINNING MENTAL HEALTH CAMPAIGNER

'I know this book will change the lives of so many people. The stories Andrea shares are honest, open and captivating to read, but at the same time full of incredible takeaways that are transformational. That combined with the practical steps she shares makes this book so impactful and one I'll read over and over again.'
CARRIE GREEN, FOUNDER OF THE FEMALE ENTREPRENEUR ASSOCIATION AND AUTHOR OF SHE MEANS BUSINESS

'An inspiring shot in the arm for any woman who wants to thrive and live her best life. It's like sitting down with an honest, kind friend who will champion you through good times and bad.'
SUZY WALKER, PSYCHOLOGIES

'A fantastic self-help double dose of adrenaline and empathy from someone who has challenged herself to the limit and really understands other women.'
VIV GROSKOP, AUTHOR OF H̶

D1418937

YOU JUST NEED TO Believe It

YOU JUST NEED TO Believe It

10 Ways in 10 Days to Unlock Your Courage and Reclaim Your Power

ANDREA McLEAN

HAY HOUSE

Carlsbad, California • New York City
London • Sydney • New Delhi

Published in the United Kingdom by:
Hay House UK Ltd, The Sixth Floor, Watson House,
54 Baker Street, London W1U 7BU
Tel: +44 (0)20 3927 7290; Fax: +44 (0)20 3927 7291
www.hayhouse.co.uk

Published in the United States of America by:
Hay House Inc., PO Box 5100, Carlsbad, CA 92018-5100
Tel: (1) 760 431 7695 or (800) 654 5126
Fax: (1) 760 431 6948 or (800) 650 5115; www.hayhouse.com

Published in Australia by:
Hay House Australia Pty Ltd, 18/36 Ralph St, Alexandria NSW 2015
Tel: (61) 2 9669 4299; Fax: (61) 2 9669 4144; www.hayhouse.com.au

Published in India by:
Hay House Publishers India, Muskaan Complex,
Plot No.3, B-2, Vasant Kunj, New Delhi 110 070
Tel: (91) 11 4176 1620; Fax: (91) 11 4176 1630; www.hayhouse.co.in

A catalogue record for this book is available from the British Library.

Tradepaper ISBN: 978-1-78817-727-6
E-book ISBN: 978-1-78817-731-3
Audiobook ISBN: 978-1-78817-728-3

Interior images: 155 Andrea McLean; 205 Nicky Johnston

Printed and bound in Great Britain by TJ Books Ltd, Padstow, Cornwall.

To all those imprisoned by your fear...
the key to your cage has been inside you all along.

Contents

Believe it can be done.
When you believe something
can be done, really believe, your
mind will find the ways to do it.
Believing a solution paves
the way to the solution.

DAVID J. SCHWARTZ

Prologue

Here are some home truths about quitting your job to follow your dreams in the middle of a global pandemic:

1. It's not as romantic as it sounds.

2. It's euphoric and terrifying at the same time.

3. No one will understand what the hell you're doing.

4. There will be days when *you'll* think, *What the hell am I doing?*

5. It will be the worst of times.

6. It will be the best of times.

7. Every day for a very long time, your overriding emotion will be fear.

8. You'll lose your carefully planned safety net.

9. Your relationships will be tested to the limit.

10. You'll wish you'd done it *years ago*.

It's August 2021 – exactly nine months since I quit my job. The job I did for 26 years; the job that saw me travel the world and experience the incredible highs of interviewing some of the most famous and influential people on the planet, as well as the lows where I'd force myself to walk through the stage door, the bright smile on my face hiding the knots of sickening dread in my stomach.

Why would someone leave a highly paid job that others would do *anything* to have? So many reasons... but in my case, it all came down to one: every day, my gut was telling me that I was in the wrong place.

And my head was telling my gut to shut up because I had (still have) bills to pay and a family to support; it was telling me that people were relying on me and that *no one* walks away from a job to follow their heart. Not just any job, either, but a high-profile one, anchoring an award-winning, ratings-grabbing national daytime TV show.

But after writing my third bestselling book, in which I'd taken all my life's learnings and poured them onto the page to help other women feel good, I realized that I needed to take my own damn advice.

A Leap of Faith

It was 2020 and the world had gone into free fall. Entire nations had ground to a halt as the planet was gripped by a pandemic that would change all our lives. My website, thisgirlisonfire.com, which had started as a simple blog two years earlier, was becoming a business run by me and my husband and co-founder, Nick, who was working flat out without a salary to keep it going.

However, this business was helping everyone *but me*. I was the breadwinner, funding the website through my other work, but I was unable to immerse myself in it fully. I wanted to give it everything I had. I wanted to jump all in. But how could I?

Then it occurred to me that there were people way smarter than me who had made decisions and business forecasts for 2020. They had meticulously planned how they thought things would go, and then BAM! The world changed and everything was whipped away from them in an instant.

And I realized that I'd been too afraid to make the leap from a job that no longer fired up my soul towards one that I *really* wanted to do. The core of a job that was in my heart when I drove to London as a 24-year-old with everything I owned on the back seat of my car, and then slept on floors and worked for free to get experience: that core was to interview people I was fascinated by and whose story could help change the lives of those who heard it.

Nick and I sat down and worked out every single thing that could go wrong if I left my job and focused on the business. It's the best thing to do when making big decisions: list every possible disaster and break down how you would respond to it. That becomes your crisis management list – your failure blueprint.

We broke it all down, we looked at our finances and we figured we could scrape together six months' worth of funds to keep us going until the business started making some kind of income. And if the business didn't work or took longer than anticipated? I mentally and practically prepared myself to sell our family home. Our projected figures, even when stripped back, looked tight (very tight) but feasible. It *could* be done. All I needed to do was *unlock my courage and reclaim my power.*

So, a few days later, I took a deep breath and made that leap. I emailed my bosses and gave them my notice, and a week later I announced on live television that I was leaving my job to pursue my dreams. I didn't intend to cry, but as the words left my mouth and I told the watching world my plans, I realized there really was no going back.

Fear engulfed every part of me. I found myself saying out loud a variation of the quote that hangs in our office at home: 'I want to do something brave. I know that I may fall, but I have to know... what if I fly?'

Immediately after I sent the email to my bosses, something inside me shifted. I felt in charge of my own destiny for the first time in a quarter of a century. And the moment I drove away after my final show – during which I'd cried with emotion as my friend and West End musical theatre star Brenda Edwards serenaded me with a rendition of 'My Girl' and they'd played a montage of all the funny, heartbreaking and inspiring moments of my two decades at ITV – I felt a weight lift.

I had a bag of clothes that the wardrobe department had let me take, a big cake, lots of farewell cards... and that was it. All I had to show for a lifetime of work. I felt light and free.

Being Myself

I left my job with its six-figure salary during a global pandemic because I saw myself in a way that others did not, simply because they'd never seen me that way. I was the safe pair of hands, the good girl, the one who never made a fuss and kept her head down and got on with the job. I was the one who did the shifts that others wouldn't, who didn't rise to confrontation, who turned the other cheek and rose above.

I left to be myself. I left because I wanted to be more. I left because I finally believed I could be more. While it took guts to leave my job, what I didn't anticipate was how much courage and self-belief I'd need, day in, day out, to keep that freedom of spirit. You see, I've been brave on many, many occasions in my life. In times of crisis, in times of emotional duress, I've kept my cool and done what I felt was best. And once that crisis subsided, I quietly dealt with whatever fallout came my way.

But this was different. There was no immediate crisis to be managed by a steady hand. Instead, it was a drip, drip, drip of fallout that turned into climbing a mountain made of sand. What kept me going wasn't simply blind faith – it was a belief in what I was capable of creating and the courage to carry on when things got tough.

It took me *years* to build up the strength to believe that I'm capable of doing what fills my soul. It took turning my back on a successful career in TV that people clamour to get into. It took ignoring the raised eyebrows of those who didn't understand why I'd make such a leap. It took holding tight and believing in my ambitions while the storms of self-doubt, exhaustion and defeat battered me from the inside out. It took getting help from experts when my relationship with the love of my life felt like it was on shaky ground.

Getting to the place where I've found happiness has meant consistently having courage and belief in myself, my actions and my attitude. And this is what I'm offering *you*: in this book I'll show you how you can find happiness too. *You just need to believe it.*

But here's the amazing part: you don't have to wait years, or even months; over just *10 days* I'll walk you through a series of challenges that will enable you to find the strength of self-belief – of *self-wonder* – that you need to feel *powerful* in the face of your fears.

I'll be passing on everything that I've learned myself, along with the wisdom of others, to help you experience your own breakthrough when it comes to moving on from being paralyzed by fear.

I *know* that you're going to feel better about yourself and your life by the time you've finished this book. I've completed these challenges with hundreds of women in my community and have watched them literally *transform* before my eyes. What you're going to do in the next 10 days *works.* You won't believe how far you can go, and how you'll be able to walk alongside your fear.

I can believe it. I've seen it. I've done it.

Now let me show *you.*

Introduction

'What you believe, you receive.'

GABBY BERNSTEIN

This book isn't about just believing that your dreams will come true, that you'll no longer be afraid and that your life will just ta-da! into wonderfulness. That would be a fairy tale or a magic trick because it's not how life works. So, let's get a few things straight before we begin, just to be sure we're starting off on the right foot...

◆ **Think of one thing that you *absolutely* believe.** Off the top of your head, go! It can be anything, good or bad. I'll wait... okay, that belief you have – whether it's that you're going to achieve an amazing dream or goal or that you're stupid and ugly and no one loves you (which isn't true by the way, and I'm going to show you why) – is the driving force behind *every single thing* that you do.

   It doesn't matter whether that belief is true or false; the very fact that you believe it is affecting every decision you make. You're already living your life by 'just believing' something – you just didn't know it! I'm going to show you how to use what you're doing already in a way that will help you.

♦ **This book isn't about quitting your job or starting a new business.** It's not about work at all. It's not about leaving a relationship, either, or moving house, or finding new friends, or climbing mountains and leaping off them, or starting a new life. It's a book about *you*. (Although you're about to find the courage to make any of those other things happen.)

♦ **No one's going to save you.** I'm not going to save you. If you believe that's all you need and are waiting for a hero or heroine to step in and make everything better, then you're going to be waiting *forever*. However, the fact that *I'm* not going to save you is a good thing because it means that *you* get to do it! I'll just be showing you how. It also means that *you get all the credit* when it works (which it does), and *you get to feel fantastic about yourself*. I'll just be feeling really, really proud of you.

♦ **Your starting point is unimportant.** It's genuinely doesn't matter what your life is like right now; even if you have absolutely nothing and are at rock bottom with no opportunities and only obstacles in front of you, this is just your point A. This is your right now, not your forever, and in this book you'll learn how to take everything that's been thrown your way and learn a lesson from it.

If you're thinking, *What the hell can you teach me? You don't know my life!* just relax. You're right, I don't, and I also don't pretend to. What you'll learn in this book comes from people all around the world at different times in our history, from past to present, who have lived lives that you and I will never know. Sometimes you learn from a teacher, and sometimes life must be the lesson. I've just taken what I've learned from others and I'm passing it on to you, along with the bits I've learned for myself. You'll be your *own* teacher, using the knowledge I'm sharing.

♦ **This book will change your life.** It absolutely will. I know this for a fact because what you're about to learn has *already* transformed the lives of the countless women who have completed the 10 Ways in 10 Days challenge – the very one on which this book is based. These women achieved incredible changes that they hadn't even realized they were capable of – once they learned that they had the power within them to unlock their courage and the belief that they could do brave things. I've spoken to them, and laughed and cried with them, as they shared their transformation stories. *This works.*

The women I'm talking about are from my This Girl Is On Fire community – my beloved founder members who joined me at the very start of my journey and are still with me today. I love them as if they're family – in fact, they're part of my TGIOF family! They've been patient, kind, loyal and honest, and in return I've taken their feedback on board and continued to overdeliver on every promise I've made to them.

I've watched them transform from nervous, quiet women who were unsure about how to make the changes they needed in their life, to confident, happy and outgoing women who are dedicated to passing on the life-changing joy of personal growth to their circle of family, loved ones and friends in a beautiful ripple effect of love.

♦ **Simply *reading* this book won't change your life.** Nope. That's like reading a cookbook then putting it back on the shelf and wondering why you still can't make duck pâté *en croûte*, or whatever it is you'd really like to be able to cook. It doesn't happen by itself – you need to try, and to work at it.

If you've ever picked up a book like this in the past and thought, *Nah, that looks like too much effort* before putting it down again, I'm guessing you're in the same state of mind you were in a year ago, five years ago, or longer. Wondering why your life hasn't changed, living in fear and lacking self-belief. It's fine if you're okay with that, but the fact that you're holding this book in your hand suggests to me that you're not. So, this time, don't put it down and walk away. Try it. Work at it. What have you got to lose?

♦ **Unlocking your courage is an *amazing* feeling.** But this doesn't mean that you won't be afraid ever again. Fear is a part of our lives for a reason – as we all know, without it we'd be running around doing some pretty stupid and probably painful things. So, while on a practical level fear stops us from doing things that may hurt us physically and mentally, it can also prevent us from living life to its fullest. Fear can make us feel pain where we don't need to.

Unlocking our courage means learning how to rationalize our fear, tame it and ultimately work with it. Why have I used the word 'unlock'? Because I believe that while our fear roams freely inside us, growling and scaring us into corners, we also have courage locked away inside us, too. I'll show you how to unlock that courage and instruct fear to walk alongside you.

Moving Beyond Our Limits

You may not think that unlocking your courage is something you can do right now. I hear you. I didn't think that in my 50s I could walk away from a career that I'd spent a quarter of a century building, putting my relationship and my home on the line! But that's the thing about believing in yourself – you realize that you *do* have it in you to do things you didn't think you could because they're uncomfortable or challenging, or indeed scary. It's a pretty scary thing to step out of our comfort zone, to shake up the status quo. What will people think? What will our husbands, our wives, our children, our friends – Oh, my God, the neighbours – make of it?

Comfort zones are strange things; what seems impossible to one person is no big deal to another. When I turned 50 there was an assumption that I'd be scribbling down a bucket list of things that I *had* to do, now that I'd arrived at the crest of the hill and the only way forwards was, apparently, down, down, down.

But what would I write on my bucket list? I've already ticked off most of the things that would be on there. I've sky-dived over Lake Taupō in New Zealand, bungee-jumped off a bridge in Australia, abseiled off Table Mountain in South Africa, trekked through the hills of northern Thailand, sat with wild gorillas in the mountains of Uganda, fallen backwards from a helicopter over the Andes Mountains in Chile (on purpose, I must add) and skinny-dipped at midnight in Cuba.

I've been married three times and I'm raising four beautiful children – two of my own and two stepchildren. My life has been full thus far, and that fullness has meant falling over, getting hurt and learning how to get back up again and let those scabs heal.

I've learned that height and speed are scary but conquerable and that past traumas don't have to define future behaviour.

And through the work I've done in writing books, training myself and helping people push through the fear that holds them back, I've learned that what *really* makes us feel as if we're out of our comfort zone is being seen for who we really are.

We all wear protective layers, whether it's our uniform for work, the smile that masks our pain or even the computers and phones we hide behind to avoid face-to-face contact. Stepping out from behind these layers – showing the world *who we really are* –

takes much more courage than hurling ourselves out of planes or down mountainsides.

You don't get told 'Well done, aren't you brave?' for taking up belly dancing or starting a new business because you've always fancied 'giving it a go', but if that's a really big deal for you, then you deserve the same amount of recognition.

Learning and Growing

In the period that followed that leap of faith away from my comfort zone of working in TV towards a world of service and growth, Nick and I were also learning how to put all the practical and psychological work we'd done, and continue to do, on ourselves into something tangible and recognizable.

Although I'd already written books on how to feel better about yourself and had a library of research books that I devoured out of passionate interest, I wanted to be sure that I was doing things the right way and to the best of my ability. My masterclasses in such subjects as 'What are the stories we tell ourselves?' and 'How to figure out what you want' were going down a storm on the website, but a part of me wanted to tick the box that said I was professionally qualified to give my thoughts on these issues.

So, Nick and I started training to become certified coaches with a lovely man called Liam James Collins, co-founder of The Coaching Masters. I did this alongside the weekly sessions I was having with a woman called Melanie from international life coach Brendon Burchard's team. I felt as if I was doing my absolute best to make myself accountable: keeping on track with my goals and talking though my fears and limiting beliefs as a client, but also learning how to help others with these same issues as a coach. It was an incredible time of learning, absorbing, building and growing.

And if I'm really honest, when I see it all written down now, I wonder how the hell I managed it! On top of trying to be a present and caring parent, a loving wife, and, oh yes, doing something just for myself every now and then.

Impossible, right? Yes, it is – if you expect it to be roaring ahead with a 100 per cent success rate in every part, all the time. That doesn't work, and sometimes Nick and I both got it really, really wrong. But we *learned* and we *grew*. How? Because we believed in what we were doing, and we didn't let the fear of how much we were taking on freeze us into inaction.

I've told you this because I want you to understand that there are so many factors in our life that we wrap up in fear – our work, our relationships, our status and our perceived success or failure are just for starters. Fear can penetrate every single aspect of our life and if we allow it to take root and take control, it can take something that's good and pure and destroy it.

I've realized that while I've shown courage in the face of life's challenges and have relished the adrenaline that scaring myself brings, this has meant that at times, my comfort zone has been pushed only within *my own* set of limits. Isn't this something we all do? But what if we let the *world* set those limits? What would we choose to say yes to then? How much courage do we possess inside us?

. . . .

**Growth of any kind means discomfort,
potential embarrassment and the high
likelihood of failure. And that's okay.**

. . . .

There's no age limit to trying to do something you've never done before, and no age restrictions on picking yourself up, dusting yourself off and starting all over again. That's why I continue to push myself beyond the limits I think I'm capable of and why I'll keep on doing so. I don't have more courage than anyone else – I'm simply endlessly curious about where my line in the sand is, and whether it's possible to consistently step over it.

Pushing Past Fear

You see, we *all* have courage inside us; we just need to know how to find it and unlock it. And that's what *you* will discover in this book, as you challenge yourself to push past your fears, whatever they are. By the time you've finished this book, you'll have learned how to do the following:

♦ Believe it – whatever your 'it' is

♦ Feel worthy of love and know that you *are* loved

♦ Understand the power of the words you use on yourself and how to replace them

♦ Reflect on your progress and commit to continue doing great things – including scaring yourself!

◆ Walk alongside fear

◆ Get organized

◆ Get accountable

◆ Break the behaviour patterns that are holding you back

◆ Set your morning and evening routine

◆ Unlock your courage and use it every day

◆ Reclaim the power that's been inside you all along

◆ Unleash your self-belief and use it in a positive way

Now that you're almost ready to get started, I want you do something for me. It may not be the kind of thing you usually do, but you've come this far, so please humour me! We're going to do a visualization that will help you whenever you feel that your fears are insurmountable and that you don't have enough courage within you to overcome them. It's a reminder that what you need to overcome fear isn't simply courage – it's *love*.

Unlock Your Courage Visualization

Imagine yourself in a cell. It's a damp, dark basement with very little light coming in through a tiny, filthy window. You're caged inside the cell and there are bars to an open space in front of you where a tiger paces up and down, up and down.

The tiger is huge: the biggest you've ever seen. It's angry, snarling, growling, squinting its eyes in the semi-darkness. It's sensitive to even the smallest action, whirling round and baring its teeth at you whenever you move.

You sit still, fixated on the tiger, watching as it stalks up and down, up and down. You've been in this cell for as long as you can remember. You don't like it and it isn't comfortable, but you're used to it. You know that provided you stay still and quiet, you'll be okay.

The key to your cell is in the lock of the cage. In the past, every time you've tentatively put your hand through the bars to turn the key to your freedom, the tiger has lunged at you, and you've flung yourself backwards, cowering, waiting for it to retreat.

Today, you look at the tiger and really study it, staring at its face as it paces back and forth. You notice for the first time that there's a beauty to its face, to its intensity. You look at it even more closely and realize with a shock that this is a female tiger; you'd assumed that due to its size and aggression, it was a male.

You think back to all the times the tiger has lunged at you and realize that she was never trying to bite you or eat you – instead, she was forcing you back inside the cage. She's never tried to get in the cage, or to get at you through the bars; she's simply been stopping you from getting out.

The tiger senses your stare, stops pacing and turns to look at you. Her eyes look deeply into yours and you see – *really* see, for the first time – that she isn't your captor but your guard. Why is she keeping guard over you? You stare into each other's eyes and the answer comes from her soul to yours.

She's protecting you. She's keeping you safe inside the cage, away from anything that could hurt you. It's her one primal goal – to keep you safe. She's a creature whose sole purpose is to be afraid of what may happen to you if you're away from her, so she must keep you close.

But you weren't meant to live in a cage, away from the outside world and the hurt and harm that it's destined to bring. You know, deep down inside, that this isn't how life is meant to be lived. But how can you change it? Keeping your eyes on the tiger, you slowly stretch your arm through the bars and reach for the key. As your fingers turn the key, the lock scrapes and the tiger turns her head. She sees what you've done and with a roar, she lunges at your arm. But this time you don't withdraw it. You shove the door open, as wide as it will go, letting it smash against the wall. There's nothing now between you and the tiger and she keeps coming at you, roaring.

The sound of the tiger's fear fills the air; it's ringing in your ears and you can feel it in your chest, in your head, in your pounding heart. You keep your eyes fixed on hers as she pounces. She lands on top of you and pins you to the floor, roaring in your face. You keep looking into her eyes and you see her anger that you've disobeyed her and her confusion as to why.

As she roars, you force yourself to feel love. You will it, push it up from the core of you – your love for this creature who's doing the one thing she's been put on this Earth to do: keep you from harm. You let the love build and flow, starting at your heart and then flowing through your body, your limbs and head and out into the room. You reach up and stroke the tiger's face, holding it with both hands, letting her feel your love and gratitude for everything she's done for you.

Gradually, the tiger's roar fades, and she stares down at you in silence before stepping back. As you get to your feet, you look down on her. She stands silent and strong beside you, waiting for instruction. You step out of your cage, and she steps with you. Beside you, close to you, ready to protect you, to fight for you, to fight alongside you. You feel her strength and love, and she feels yours.

You are joined now. She is Fear, and she'll always be by your side. You are Courage, and you'll always be by her side. Together, you'll conquer the world and everything it brings you. You know it. You believe it. This is your story. It's time to reclaim your power.

Make a Promise to Yourself

*'Being brave isn't the absence of fear. Being brave
is having that fear but finding a way through it.'*
BEAR GRYLLS

'm excited about you doing this 10-day challenge because I know what's in store for you and I know how incredible you're going to feel at the end of it. This experience has the potential to change your life in every single way. Are you ready for that?

The first thing you need to know is that this isn't a quick fix where, just like that in 10 days' time, your life will be awesome, everything you believe in and wish for will have come true and you'll be a superhero and live happily ever after. No. This isn't a movie.

Over the next 10 days, you'll learn how to unlock the courage that's hidden away inside of you, but that's not all. You'll also learn just how *worthy* you are of all the good things that life has in store for you, how *strong* you are, how *lovable* you are, and how *loved* you are.

And you'll learn how to face the challenges in your life in the way that best serves *you*. Because we're all different and the challenges and fears we face are as unique as we are. That's why you'll be doing this work on your own. Taking the time to really think about what it is you're facing and what you want to achieve by overcoming it. In fact, there will be a lot of thinking over the next 10 days, and through that you'll learn how to unleash your self-belief and reclaim your power.

Getting Started

While you're working with the book, you'll need four things:

♦ **A journal.** I'm a *huge* believer in the practice of journalling: writing down our thoughts and feelings in order to understand them more clearly. I believe there's a direct link between the words that pour out of our brain and onto the page and the structure we then start putting together to change our thought patterns, habits and behaviour. Journalling can also help make your dreams come true because if you think it and write it, you can make it happen!

In each chapter, under the heading *Journal Time*, you'll find questions to ask yourself and other content designed to help you get to know yourself and your life better. Write down your responses to these in a journal or a notebook – or type them into a document on your laptop if you prefer. Whatever works best for you.

♦ **A friend.** Choose someone to go on this journey with you, a bravery buddy if you like. Knowing that there's someone who will champion you when you make a breakthrough and cheer you on when you don't feel like doing the work will be a big help. *And* you'll have someone to celebrate with when, at the end of the 10 days, you've unlocked your courage, broken through your fear, felt yourself becoming brave and are excited about what the future holds for you.

♦ **A commitment to doing what's asked of you over the next 10 days.** No one else can do this challenge for you, and that's *great news* because it means that *only you* will have the breakthrough and feel on top of the world when, after 10 days, you're fired up, brave and ready to go out and get exactly what you want out of this one precious life we're given. No one else – just *you*.

♦ **The You Just Need to Believe It playlist.** This free playlist features uplifting music that will get you charged up! Simply search for You Just Need to Believe It on Spotify and off you go! Why a playlist? Well, it's been scientifically proven that music has the power to change our mood, to give us energy when we lack it and to calm us down when we feel overwhelmed. Every song on this playlist has been specifically chosen to lift your mood and inspire you, so I recommend listening to it while you're working out, commuting, or just keeping busy around the house.

Music is also a very powerful tool for evoking memory and recall, so if you listen to the playlist as you read the book, hearing the songs subsequently will spark strong recollections of the lessons you're learning – taking you instantly to a place where you feel brave and filled with self-belief.

Your First Steps

Are you ready to take the first steps in unlocking the courage you have buried away inside you? Are you ready to start believing in yourself, your abilities and the great things that you're capable of doing? Wonderful! Let's begin.

Step 1: Your Promise to Yourself

In your journal/notebook, write out the following statement:

I [insert your name] promise to commit 30 minutes a day to investing in my incredible self by completing the You Just Need to Believe It: 10 Ways in 10 Days to Unlock Your Courage and Reclaim Your Power Challenge.

I promise to be honest with myself about the fear that's holding me back, to follow the guidance given to me, and to make the changes necessary to remove negative patterns of thought and behaviour.

I understand that I'll have to face some uncomfortable feelings and that this is part of my journey towards overcoming them. If this experience awakens feelings that are too difficult for me to navigate on my own, I promise to seek help from friends or professionals who can support me.

I congratulate myself for believing that I can do this. I'm
dedicated to spending the next 10 days facing my fear, so that
I can unlock my courage and learn everything I need to believe
in myself!

Now add your signature and date it.

Step 2: Get Organized

In your paper diary or on your phone, set a daily reminder to spend
30 minutes a day working on yourself. Get up 30 minutes earlier
each day if that's the only way you can make the time. But *do*
make it – this is *you time* and it's precious, so protect it.

Get out your journal/notebook/laptop – you're going to be
using it every day during your 30 minutes to write about
your *aims*, your *thoughts*, your *dreams*, your *hopes* and your
achievements as you complete the 10-day challenge. Especially
your achievements! Every tiny step you make will bring you closer
to overcoming the fear that's holding you back from living a
life you love. If you start paying attention to the progress you're
making each day, you'll begin to truly believe in yourself and
stop self-limiting.

Step 3: Get Accountable

If we don't tell anyone about the promises that we've made to
ourselves, we find it easy to put them on the shelf – *so tell people*
about this promise.

You have two choices here, depending on how you're feeling. You can either put out a post on your social media (Facebook or Instagram are good to start with, and if you're in the This Girl Is On Fire app, let us cheer you on!) or send a message to close, trusted friends telling them you've made a decision to change your life forever and that for the next 10 days you're going to do something every day to help you become stronger, braver and so unbelievably *fired up* about how much better your life's going to be!

Tell your friends to put a reminder in their phones to contact you after 10 days to ask how you got on. Now, I know exactly what you're thinking: *But what if I don't finish the 10 days? I'll need to have awkward conversations and make excuses about why I didn't complete the challenge.*

Stop that thought right now. You are the one in control here, and the only reason you won't complete this 10-day challenge is that you don't want it enough. This is about *you* feeling good about yourself; this is about *you* unlocking your courage. So, get excited about the conversations you're going to have with your friends once you've succeeded. Here's what your post/message should say:

'Hi everyone, for the next 10 days I'm going to be doing something incredible: learning how to be brave! Starting today, I'm going to figure out what I want out of life, learn how to stop being afraid to try and stop making excuses about why I feel stuck where I am. At the end of the 10 days, I'll have unlocked my courage and started to feel brave and excited about what the future holds.

I'm really looking forward to doing this, and I'd like your help. Please put a reminder in your phone to ask me in 10 days' time what changes I've made to my life. That's it. YOU are my accountability partner and knowing that you're going to ask me this question will give me the determination to keep going. I'll speak to you in 10 days.'

Congratulations! I know that was scary – just the *thought* of putting this message out into the world is terrifying – but you did it!

***

I'll see you tomorrow, when we'll begin by looking into what makes you 'you' by listening to the story you've been telling yourself about who you are and what you're capable of doing in life. By the end of Day 2, you'll see that whatever you *think* you're capable of is just the tip of the iceberg! You're *amazing*, and I'm going to show you why *you just need to believe it*.

Dᴀʏ 2

Tell Yourself a Different Story

'Change your story, change your life.'
Dᴇᴇᴘᴀᴋ Cʜᴏᴘʀᴀ

Today is when we really start to do some work on ourselves. I think you're going to find this fascinating because it's all about *you*! You may think that you're pretty clued-up about who and what you are, but I guarantee that by the end of the day your mind will have been blown by what you've learned about yourself. You'll know why you think the way you do and see that you've been telling yourself the same story repeatedly for so long, you believe that's all there is to you. I'm here to tell you that there's so much more!

We're going to look at ways to stop the unhelpful narrative that's been playing in your head and crank up the volume on the helpful narrative. You'll also see why this is one of the most important life lessons that any of us will ever learn. By the time you've finished this chapter you'll understand that just because you've told yourself something (or someone else has), that doesn't have to become the story of your life.

> **You're in control. You're writing your story
> and you're living it. No one else.**

Entrepreneur and founder of Spanx underwear Sarah Blakely puts it another way. (If you don't follow Sarah on social media, then I'd urge you to: she's funny, warm and whip-smart – some of my favourite qualities in a human.) She posted the following statement on her Instagram, and to me it was especially pertinent as I saw it while I was writing this chapter! For context, the post followed a photo of Sarah drinking from a mug saying: 'If your own story isn't inspiring to you, it's time to re-write that sh*t.'

'You are the director of your own life. One day, after selling fax machines door-to-door for 7 years, I pulled off the side of the road and made a decision to change my life. I set intentions, I wrote down goals, I visualized my life differently and then I got busy changing it... one day at a time. I don't know where you are in your life right now, [but] just know that at any time you can pull over and re-write that s*%+. It's your life, it's your story. Make it a good one.'

If You Believe It, It Becomes So

Now I know that in this book, we aren't talking specifically about being an entrepreneur, but I think Sarah's words are worth paying attention to because they underline the idea that the stories we tell ourselves, and the narrative that we then live out, control our destiny because we *choose* to believe them.

Yes, of course, much of what happens to us in life is beyond our control; however, the way we *react* to those things is one hundred per cent within our control. This isn't to say that you have to laugh in the face of disaster and terrible loss – of course not, that would be ridiculous. There will be times in your life when things happen to you that are truly awful and painful, and during those times you need to do what you can to survive them with all the love and support you can find.

I'm talking about when life's bumpy – when it isn't feeling the way you'd like it to feel or working out as you'd wish. As Sarah says, it's time to rewrite that shit – beginning with what's going on inside your own head.

We need to remember that most of what's going on in our head stems from our beliefs about who we are. But where do we get these ideas in the first place? Are we born instinctively knowing who we are? Not really – we're born looking for support and reassurance from our caregivers and we base our sense of worth on how they treat us.

If we're fortunate enough to have parents or other caregivers who love us and treat us kindly and well, then it makes sense for us to assume that we're a person who deserves to be treated kindly and well. But if we're unfortunate and have caregivers who don't do this, we grow up with a sense that we're not worthy of the love and tenderness that others seem to receive. Very little of this behaviour has to do with *us*.

As we grow older, our self-perception is further driven by our surroundings and our peers – some of whom we'll never actually meet but who nevertheless have a huge impact on our self-esteem via their 'likes' or otherwise of what we post on social media. Are we 'unlikeable' if we're not 'liked'? These are issues that once would have been limited to our family and circle of friends but are now literally in the hands of strangers.

The Looking-Glass Self

One of the most popular articulations of this phenomenon was made by the American sociologist Charles Horton Cooley. At the start of the 20th century, long before social media was a twinkle in an inventor's eye, he wrote: 'I am not who you think I am. I am not who I think I am. I am who I think you think I am.'

That's a *lot* of over-thinking! It's also such a neat summing-up of what we do every single day in any given moment. Cooley's words appear in his 1902 work *Human Nature and the Social Order*, and they reveal how little we've changed in the last 120 years.[1] We're still telling ourselves stories about who we are that are based on what we think *others* think of us.

When Cooley wrote about this idea, that the way we think of ourselves is inextricably woven into how we think we're seen by others, he was examining a concept called the 'looking-glass self'. Let's put it this way...

You meet up with a group of friends and during the conversation you notice that a couple of them aren't engaging with you in the way they normally do. They seem a little distant and appear to be glancing at each other every time you speak. You instantly feel self-conscious. *Do I sound stupid?* you ask yourself. *They definitely think I sound stupid.* So, you stop speaking and drift into silence, convinced that these friends hate you.

Now let's flip that scenario around. You're telling an anecdote to the group of friends, and everyone's laughing and engaged. You think you're the wittiest person in the room. I'm sure we all know someone who's so socially clueless that they fall on one side or the other of this scenario; however, it has very little to do with how great they are or aren't.

I have a friend who leaves every party *convinced* that they've been funny, smart and engaging and that everyone loves them. They're completely deaf and blind to the fact that they insulted one person by laughing at them and annoyed another by pointing out a mistake in their story; they also didn't notice a single eye-roll while they talked loudly and self-importantly about what they'd been up to.

This person thinks they're amazing because *that's the story* they've been telling themselves and they wholeheartedly believe it. This is lovely for them, but really, their story is just as untrue as the story of the person who's crippled by social anxiety and thinks they're a waste of space because they spotted someone yawning in their company. What's so fascinating here is that the truth of the story has nothing to do with its power – if you believe it, it becomes so. Therefore, it's *so important* to be careful about the words that we use when talking both *to* ourselves and *about* ourselves.

The Director of Our Own Life

The stories we tell ourselves have a *huge* impact on how we live our lives. They can make us calm and confident, empathetic and loving, engaging and wise, or they can cripple us with insecurity or make us a social bore. We know that we live our lives through the reflection of others' opinions of us – whether they're true or false. However, *we* have the power to decide what our story is, even though we don't often feel it.

'Imagination is always manufacturing scenarios, both good and bad, and the ego tries to keep you trapped in the multiplex of the mind... Our eyes are not viewers, they're also projectors that are running a second story over the picture that we see in front of us all the time. Fear is writing that script, and the working title is: "I'll Never Be Enough."'[2]

These words were spoken by the American actor Jim Carrey during a speech at Maharishi International University in the USA in 2014. Jim Carrey? The rubber-faced comedian who's made generations of people laugh? Yes. Because he's also Jim Carrey whose family was made homeless for a time during his teens, who worked hard to help provide for his parents and siblings, and who told himself that it was 'his job' to make his parents feel good about themselves.

Carrey later broadened out that job description to the rest of the world; during his speech he revealed that at the age of 28 he realized that his life's purpose was to 'free people from concern', which was why he wanted to make everyone laugh and forget their troubles for a while. That was the story he told himself; he believed it and lived by it for many years, and it made him feel good. Until it didn't any more.

How do we make sure that the story we tell ourselves is one that makes us feel good? Not necessarily in a global movie star way, or as I mentioned earlier, in an insensitive social bore at a party way. I mean in a way that serves us – that makes us feel whole.

We reframe it.

Reframing Our Story

Cast your mind back to the summer of 2021, when the UK was half in half out of lockdown, there were protests on the streets of London about Covid vaccines, face masks and travelling abroad, and everyone was angry and upset. And then the UEFA European Football Championship, the Euros, began.

At first, it was only football fans who were interested in the tournament – after all, the rest of us thought, we've been here so many times before and it's always the same: lots of media hype and frenzy and everyone getting over-excited; and then the British teams lose, and we all just carry on with our lives.

But this time around, for a while, it was different, and not simply because of the players in the England and Scotland national teams, who are always dedicated and talented sportsmen. No, it was because of the England team's manager, Gareth Southgate OBE.

Gareth is a player-turned-manager who experienced a career low back in 1996 when his infamous missed penalty against Germany in the semi-final of the Euros saw the England team knocked out of the tournament. All his years as a successful footballer, working his way up through the ranks, training hard with the England team, playing well throughout the tournament, seemed to count for nothing at that moment and in the years that followed.

He became an icon of failure in football, the photo of his shocked, downturned face appearing in the sports pages every time the Euros came around. It was as if that one moment in a young player's life was responsible for every occasion the England team were knocked out of a tournament. It wasn't just that Gareth Southgate took it personally – the whole country took it personally, and they wouldn't let it lie.

Speaking in August 2020, a few months into the coronavirus pandemic, with the President-Designate of the Football Association, Prince William, Duke of Cambridge, as part of the 'Heads Up' mental health campaign, Gareth explained his thoughts[3]:

'Without doubt, when I look back, that was professionally the most challenging experience that I've been through... When you've messed things up, as I have, and you realize that professionally that's probably as difficult as you're going to face, it almost liberates you to say: "Right, okay, let's just attack life."'

We have to face those things. We can't hide from them. I can't hide from the fact that that happened. And then I have a decision and a choice as to how I approach dealing with it. Time has given me the opportunity to put that into better perspective. What we've just lived through for the last three months, as an example. Where does missing a penalty kick actually have any importance in the overall scheme of life?'

Preparing for Failure

That missed penalty kick could have been Gareth's story. Like many footballers before and after him, he could have drowned in the sea of 'what if' and 'what could have been'. But he didn't. He chipped away at himself in a positive way rather than a negative one, which could have been expected.

When he became the manager of the England national team in 2016, he worked hard at filling in the gaps in his knowledge and continually looked forwards. He surrounded himself with people from whom he could learn – experts and leaders in other sports such as Formula One and rugby – becoming aware of the different thought processes behind team building and tactics.

He read books and listened to podcasts about human behaviour and growth; he educated himself about the needs and wants of his diverse team, making sure that every element within it felt seen, heard and valued. He encouraged his players to do the same: to treat everyone they came into contact with as an equal part of their collective; to treat everyone as vital to the smooth running of the machine, no matter how small or how big and shiny.

Just as manners, learning, dedication and conviction were the habits that Gareth instilled in the England team, he also drove home the need to prepare for difficulty and failure, as those moments will always come.

The work that Gareth did on himself following his experience in the 1996 Euros didn't only serve him well and bring the England team to its first final in a major tournament for 55 years, it also made him the perfect manager to comfort his distraught players Marcus Rashford, Jadon Sancho and Bukayo Saka, who sadly repeated history, missing penalties that saw the team's dream of winning the 2020 Euros (played in the summer of 2021 due to the pandemic) disappear.

No one else could have given these young men the support and encouragement that Gareth Southgate did, from his place of knowing how difficult the coming months would be for them. Within 24 hours Gareth went from England hero to once again facing the boiling wrath of angry fans – this time as a manager with the ability to comfort and support his players.

Rethinking the Unhelpful Narrative

Failure, as we all know, is inevitable. However, the way we *react* to failure, the story we tell ourselves about it and what we choose to do with that experience, is not. Sometimes, the story you're experiencing – the one from your past that you're telling yourself now – isn't the one you're destined to be telling in your future.

**One day, your mess will be your message
of strength – that will be your story.**

How does this relate to you and the journey you're on? It's all about the back story that you believe in and whether you've made it useful or not useful. Have you ever asked yourself whether your belief that you can't do a difficult thing is based on the fact you failed at it in the past?

What about the times when you attempted something difficult, kept going and succeeded? If you dig around in your memory banks, you'll find an example of a time when you tried to do something and although it was hard, you learned how to do it; you practised it and at some point, you mastered it.

It could have been something simple like riding a bike or something frightening like learning to swim. Perhaps it was following a complicated recipe or becoming fluent in a foreign language. Rethink your narrative that you can't do difficult things – inside you is a memory that will give you the proof you need that you've done difficult things before, and you can do them again.

Journal Time ✍

Consider the following questions and in your journal write your responses:

1. How would you describe your younger self?

Think about how your life was before reality in some cases and insecurity in others kicked in; before you realized that your dream might be tougher to achieve than you thought or was unrealistic or just plain silly. When it was *your* dream, and it was wonderful!

2. What story did you tell yourself when you were young?

Consider these questions, then grab your journal/notebook and write down your thoughts. It's a good way to take a trip down memory lane anyway and remind yourself of who you were back then.

3. Whatever happened to that person? Why did they change?

The answer to that is usually simple: the optimism that many of us had when we were younger was chipped away by the words used towards us by a) people who didn't have our best interests at heart; b) people who were well meaning but misguided; c) people we didn't even know who certainly didn't have our best interests at heart (hello again, social media).

Only very rarely do we simply decide for ourselves to change how we see things; mostly, we either misinterpret how we think we're seen (as in the looking-glass self) or we're told directly by others that they don't like what we're doing, so we change in order to belong.

. . . .

Stories That Don't Serve Us

Now that you're a grown-up, let's have a look at some of the stories you're telling yourself today that aren't serving you. This doesn't mean that the stories you tell yourself have to be true – they don't! For example, you don't know for sure that your idea for a new business will be a success, or that you're going to meet the person of your dreams, but telling yourself so helps you manifest it, which is *hugely* helpful!

No, I'm talking about the stories you tell yourself which bring you down and have no place in your life. Let's start with the words you use when you talk to yourself.

Journal Time ✍

In your journal, write down your response to these questions:

1. What words do you use to describe yourself, to yourself?

2. What's the story you tell others about yourself?

3. What are the stories you tell yourself about others?

This could be a family member, a best friend, or someone you've recently met and don't know very well.

This will take a while to dig into, as you may never have sat down with this version of your life before. It's a fascinating exercise, though, because it highlights the discrepancies between how you speak *to* yourself and how you speak *of* yourself, and it also reveals the stories you make up in your head about other people. Are these stories that you've created about other people true, or not? How do you know for sure?

Ask yourself and be prepared for some uncomfortable answers. Uncomfortable because you'll realize you've simply been gossiping with yourself and have no idea if the slander you're spreading inside your head is true or false. All you know is that it's been making you feel terrible. What a waste of your precious time!

The Stories You Tell Yourself

> *'Never say anything about yourself you*
> *do not want to come true.'*
> Brian Tracy

Have a think about this – what do you constantly and consistently say about yourself, both out loud and internally? I had to *unlearn* many of the stories I ended up telling myself – about my past relationships and the behaviour I experienced at the hands of others. At the time 'gaslighting' was something done in the olden days to turn on our streetlights! But now it's a term that refers to the drip-feeding of poison and self-doubt that some people in our lives do to keep us feeling insecure and unsure of ourselves.

For many years, the story I told myself was that I was unlovable, undeserving of happiness and undeserving of success but also worthless without it. I know now that none of those things is true, but they were drip-fed into my consciousness for so long they became the story I told myself.

Journal Time ✑

I think that you'll recognize a lot of the sentiments listed below because they're what so many women have shared with me through the work I do. They aren't an easy read; they're painful and sad because these are the stories that we tell ourselves day in, day out, and the truth is we end up believing them.

Read each one out loud and imagine that you're hearing someone you love saying it about *themselves*. Allow yourself to experience the sadness and the empathy you'd feel for that person.

♦ 'I'm no good at this.'

♦ 'I'm useless.'

♦ 'I'm not worth it.'

♦ 'I don't deserve it.'

♦ 'I'm only worthy if I'm successful.'

♦ 'I need to keep busy because stopping is lazy.'

♦ 'I can't say no because then people won't like me.'

♦ 'I don't mind (when you really do).'

♦ 'I can't say how I feel because other people won't like it.'

♦ 'I get everything wrong.'

♦ 'Everyone else's life is better than mine.'

♦ 'I feel judged.'

♦ 'It's just how I am.'

♦ 'It's how our family are.'

♦ 'I can't help it.'

♦ 'I'm no good at confrontation.'

♦ 'I don't deserve love.'

♦ 'I'm not lovable.'

♦ 'I always say the wrong thing.'

♦ 'I'm too loud.'

♦ 'I'm too quiet.'

♦ 'I'm so clumsy.'

These are the stories you're telling *yourself*. I'd like you to write in your journal/notebook which of these stories resonated with you. Then underneath, write down *why* you think you feel this way. Where has this come from? Yourself, or someone else?

Well done for doing that – I know it will have brought up a lot of uncomfortable feelings and memories. Be kind to yourself right now; this isn't an easy thing to do and you're doing so well to let it out. I promise that this is going to get easier!

Now let's look at *why* we tell ourselves these stories that don't serve us.

....

Why We Make Stuff Up about Ourselves

We *all* make stuff up about ourselves – it's part of our natural human behaviour. But what's so sad about this is that the story we tell ourselves is often one of lack, failure and discontent.

We do this so frequently, in fact, that this voice becomes the narrator of our own private movie, telling us repeatedly how badly we're doing, how much we're failing and how we don't deserve good things in our life. This narration moves us to live out what we hear, and unconsciously we become the director of our own reality as we focus our energy and actions on our pain and negativity.

'What you believe you receive.' – Gabby Bernstein

'Where focus goes, energy flows.' – Tony Robbins

'If you want it, you need to believe it!' – Andrea McLean

Do you see where I'm going with this? We all instinctively follow this pattern of thinking, but rather than believing in something good, possible or positive, we drive ourselves crazy by telling ourselves ridiculous stories that keep us stuck.

But why? What's the point? When we tell ourselves something, subconsciously we always cast ourselves as the hero or the victim. We rarely tread the middle ground. This is because we make our decisions emotionally and then use our rational mind to justify them to ourselves. In other words, we tell ourselves stories.

Think of the story we tell ourselves when a relationship ends. How many of us retell that tale with ourselves as the victim, or the hero? And the ex is *always* the villain! Okay, sometimes they really are the villain and we're better off without them. But every single time? Come on... really? It's okay if you've done this – we've all done it – but it's time to be really honest now about the story you've told yourself.

Journal Time ✐

Think of a time when you told yourself a story to make yourself the hero or the victim, consciously or unconsciously, in a bid to get sympathy or praise. What happened? Why did it happen? Write it down. No judgement – no one else will see it.

This story you're telling yourself right now – is it true, or is it just something you've told yourself so often that you believe it's true, or have made it true? Whatever your story (or stories) was, look at the reasons you've written and have a re-think.

Ask yourself: *Is this story really true or is it something I've told myself so often that I've made myself believe it's true?*

You'll instinctively know the answer to this; your gut will tell you whether it's a resolute yes or no. If the answer is yes, ask yourself again whether you know for absolute certain that this story is true.

Think back on the event (if that's where your story stems from) and close your eyes. Try to look at it from above, from an outsider's perspective, rather than the perspective you're accustomed to – through your own line of vision. What happened? Try to be as dispassionate as you can about this and don't let the emotions you've associated with this event overrun your recollection of it.

Once you've gone through it all, ask yourself: *Where would I be without this story?* Write down what comes to mind.

This is an extremely powerful way of figuring out whether you're hanging on to your story, as told through your eyes and heart, as a way of justifying your behaviour at the time or afterwards. After the event, it's way easier to paint yourself in a light that benefits you – as either the victim or the hero of the piece. But is it true?

I hope you're starting to see that just because you've been telling yourself something, or you've been told something many times, it doesn't mean it's true.

Now I want you to do something you may never have tried before: turn your story on its head. Could it be that what you've been saying to yourself is the *opposite* of the truth? Ask yourself: *Could the opposite be true?* This won't sit easily with you and your first reaction will be to fight it. But give it a go. Try it on for size – you're simply browsing, and this may not fit. But wouldn't it be interesting if it did?

Now write down the story again, but from the perspective that the opposite was true: that *you* were the villain of the piece. *How does that feel?* Could this be closer to the truth? Could it be *as true* as your original story? Could there be truth in *both sides* to this?

Don't feel bad about yourself, or stupid or guilty, if you see that you could have got it wrong – *this is a great moment for you!* How often do you get to let go of something that's been filling you with draining negativity?

Write down how you feel and what you think you might do with this new information. You don't need to do anything at all; you could just sit with it. But if you know in your heart that you've made a mistake, keep it in your mind that acknowledging this to the other person or people involved could be a powerful tool in stepping forwards. However, that's something that only you can decide for yourself, and there's no judgement here. Today is all about you.

Letting Go of Our Old Stories

Most of the stories we tell ourselves about things that have happened in our past aren't *us* any more and they don't serve us. I'll give you an example of this. For many years, I felt like a complete failure because I've been married three times. I'd be the one to joke about it because I felt I needed to get in there first so I wouldn't be hurt.

We all do this, don't we? We bring up what we feel is the elephant in the room – whether it's an aspect of our physical appearance, or our job, or our relationship status, whatever. It took me a long time to accept that my relationship status isn't my whole truth – it's just other people's opinion of it that was soaked into my subconscious and *became* my story.

These days, perhaps because I don't even think about it any more, if it's ever mentioned I don't feel that I must explain, justify or joke about it. It's my life experience and that's it. Whatever your past story is, let go of judgment and let it be. Don't tell your story to protect your ego, or to make yourself the victim or hero, just be *you*.

Why We Make Stuff Up about Others

Our brain relies on past experiences, and it creates positive or negative emotions related to those experiences. This explains why we find ourselves inexplicably drawn to a particular person – they remind us of someone with whom we had a good past experience. It can be something small, such as the fact they wear the same fragrance as that person did or find the same things funny; it doesn't matter what it is – something in your brain clicks in to say, *Hey, I like them!*

And it can happen the other way round, too: when we take a dislike to someone even if we barely know them or haven't had much interaction with them. We then tell ourselves a story to justify why we feel that way, and that's it. They could be the sweetest person in the world, and yet we simply won't entertain the idea of liking them.

This is because of something called unconscious bias. Our brain looks for hooks to attach to an experience. We do this every single day without even noticing it, and bit by bit we build up stories that we casually reinforce over time, without there ever having to be cold, hard facts involved. You already believe it, and therefore that makes it so.

Why do we tell ourselves stories?

♦ To protect our feelings.

♦ To prove ourselves right.

♦ To make ourselves feel better.

♦ To make things seem more exciting, or worse, than they really are, so that we can be either the hero or the victim of the tale.

Remember this the next time you're drawn to someone or repelled by them. What's their truth? And does it have anything to do with the story your brain has attached to them?

Think of a time when you made a decision about someone based on a feeling or told yourself a story about them which turned out to be untrue. Did you feel let down because they weren't who you thought they were? Maybe they never were that person – maybe *you* put the labels on them, *you* made up the story and then got upset because they didn't play it out as you'd scripted it.

What's Your Real Story?

We're going to begin this section with a simple but profound technique that I heard the international life coach Brendon Burchard use in a podcast. I was inspired to look into it more deeply, and if I'm honest, it was this technique that eventually led me down the path of training to become a life coach myself. In a similar way to the looking-glass concept I mentioned earlier, it asks us to look at ourselves through different mirrors.

Journal Time ✍

Grab your journal/notebook and do the following:

1. Write down three words that you'd use to describe yourself to someone who doesn't know you and you simply need to sum up what you're like.

2. Now write down three words that a friend who loves you would use to describe you.

3. Look at the *differences* between those two groups of words. What are they, and more importantly, *why* are they different? What is it that someone who loves you sees in you that you don't see in yourself? How can you bridge that gap? What things could you do to see yourself in the way that someone who loves you sees you?

I decided to use this technique again today, as I'm writing this, and I found it just as difficult as before! Those three words change depending on my mood: if I'm feeling confident and sparky or shy and insecure; I'm all these things, but not all at once. My three words could range from *Determined, Loyal, Genuine* to *Shy, Introverted, Nerdy*.

This time, I closed my eyes, and as if plucking names out of a hat, I went for *Strong, Loving, Centred*. Out of curiosity, and to see how close or different the words would be, I've just asked my husband which three words he'd use to describe me, and right away he said, *Generous, Kind, Beautiful* (which was very nice of him, obviously!).

But it was good to see how far I've come in my own journey with this technique; to know that I've learned to see myself in the way that those who love me see me. Trust me, it hasn't always been this way! Bear in mind that the same thing will happen to you when it comes to thinking of your three words, and that's okay. This is just where you are right now, and it's a good enough place to start.

• •

Finding Your Truth

We all have perceptions of ourselves, stories that we tell ourselves, for reasons that for much of the time we don't even understand. Perhaps it's a form of protection so we aren't hurt – think of the tiger prowling around outside your cage, keeping you inside it. Perhaps it's a role we play to help us survive a difficult or traumatic experience – think of Jim Carrey becoming the joker to provide moments of comfort to his homeless family.

Ask yourself: *Who am I when I'm not being what someone else needs me to be?* By this, I mean when you aren't behaving in a way that you've decided others need you to be. For example, as the supportive friend or the life and soul of the party.

Answering this question might feel very difficult because it may have been a very long time since you stopped and thought about yourself as a unique being in your own right, rather than as an extension of someone else's life – a daughter, son, parent, partner, friend, neighbour. *Who are you?*

> **To move away from the story you're telling yourself, you need to connect with the you who isn't telling a story: the 'you' who's just being.**

I need to be honest here and tell you that the first time I asked myself *Who am I when I'm not being what someone else needs me to be?* I cried. I found it really painful to open up to myself and look at who I am when I'm not being something for someone else, and you'll very likely feel the same. It can feel selfish, self-centred and greedy.

I'd just come out the other side of an incredibly difficult time – it was exactly a year since I'd had a breakdown, and while I'd had counselling and help and was in a much better place, I still didn't feel quite 'myself' because I didn't know who 'myself' was without doing all the things that had led to my fall. I'd burned out because I'd been trying so hard to hold myself together and be all the things that the people around me needed me to be.

So, I took a solo holiday for the first time in my life. Not a spa break with a friend, nope: I booked a week on a remote island off the coast of England. I packed notebooks, my laptop and a rucksack, and I spent hours hiking around the island, staring at the sea, listening to music on my headphones, journalling and crying.

It doesn't sound like a lot of fun, but it was my own kind of therapy – letting go of old stories I'd been telling myself about who I thought I was, or who I should be. It got to the core of who I, Andrea, really am. It was one of the bravest things I've ever done; even going away on my own was daunting, as I didn't have the excuse of 'it's for work'.

I was putting my needs first, and that took some getting used to. But that short time alone marked the beginning of the change for me. It led to me really digging into what I want, and it made me believe that I have the courage within me to do it.

Journal Time ✍

I appreciate that taking time out to be on your own is quite a drastic thing to do, and that you'll have to find your own version of it – even if it's shutting yourself away in your bedroom with a Do Not Disturb sign on the door!

Find your own place of stillness and quiet and in your journal, respond to the following questions. Just write whatever comes into your head; don't think about how the words might look or sound to anyone else: this is for *you*. It's a simple exercise but incredibly powerful. Open yourself up to whatever comes out.

Ask yourself: *When do I feel most at peace and connected with myself?*

Acknowledge that there are different sides to you: some quiet, some more energetic. When do you feel most at peace and connected with yourself? What are you doing when you feel this way? Where are you?

Now ask yourself: *What's my unique quality? What makes me different to everyone else?* Not the story that you've been telling yourself, or which others have been telling you. What's *your* truth?

For me, it's that I feel more, I see more, I care more. I feel people's energy. I feel when they're nervous or afraid and I'm drawn to help. I'm quiet and still, but I also have an energized self. I like to absorb quietly, but I also like to shine and share.

I see myself as like the moon and the sun: I'm both things. And what's interesting is that when I look back on how I was as a child, as a young teenager, I can see that so many of those qualities were there. They've always been there – I just told myself otherwise because of my life experiences. We're never anything other than what we've truly always been.

I may not be a firefighting nun who dates film stars, which was what I wanted to be when I was young, but I'm a woman who's dedicating her life to helping others; a woman who has a sense of her own spirituality and has the love of a good man by her side. My life may not look exactly how I thought it would, but my story has come true.

What are you? You're not one thing, you're many. And by constantly telling yourself one story about yourself you're missing the beauty of the rest of you.

Tell Yourself a Different Story Challenge

The next time you find yourself automatically sliding into your old story, reframe it to this:

♦ 'I'm going to make time for myself.'

♦ 'I need to look after myself so that I can care for others even better than before.'

♦ 'I'm no good at this right now... but I'll learn.'

♦ 'I'm no clumsier than anyone else.'

♦ 'I'm not useless.'

♦ 'I'm worth it.'

♦ 'I deserve it.'

♦ 'I'm worthy – regardless of how I seem to anyone else.'

Journal Time ✍

Now, in your journal, rewrite your story, in your own voice: the one you had before age, cynicism, sadness and bad experiences made you think differently about yourself. What's your story *now*?

Well done for completing today – it was the first real day of working on yourself and it may have been an uncomfortable experience for you. I'm so proud that you've committed to doing this because I know that in just a few days' time you'll be staggered by how far you've come.

You've done so well to look into yourself and to scrutinize the words you were using to describe yourself. You've examined why you were doing this to yourself and to others. You now understand that your story from your past doesn't have to be the story of your future. You know that your unique qualities are what make you the beautiful person you are... And *that's* your true story.

Each night from now on, say to yourself, *I believe I'm*.... For example, you could say: *I believe I'm courageous. I believe I'm lovable. I believe I'm loved.* Repeat those statements to remind yourself of just how incredible you really are. *If you believe it, you'll transform your life.*

You may also like to write down these statements and put them somewhere you can see them, to remind you every day. A simple way to see them regularly is to write them in the notes section of your phone, then screen shot it and make it your screensaver. Then you can carry them with you always.

Tomorrow we'll be looking at the little patterns of behaviour that you've built up over time – the ones which are having a huge impact on your life without you even realizing it. See you then!

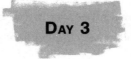

Change Your Habits

> *'Courage, like fear, is a habit. The more you do it, the more you do it, and this habit of stepping up, of taking action, more than anything else, will move you in a different direction.'*
>
> TONY ROBBINS

saw an Instagram post today that made me laugh out loud. It was from a famous young influencer who posts regularly about her life and is as refreshingly honest about her 'behind the scenes' difficulties as she is about her shiny, privileged existence.

She was having her ears pierced and asked her boyfriend to film it. What made me, and everyone else who watched the video, laugh, was how ridiculously scared she was! She flinched and screamed with fear every time the woman doing the piercing came close to her; even a tissue brushing against her face sent her into meltdown.

It was very endearing and funny to watch, but it also struck me as revealing. You see, so much of the time our attitude towards things that frighten us can make them into a much bigger deal than they need to be. However, because we've become accustomed to reacting to them in the way we do, that pattern of behaviour becomes our 'normal'.

I know this young influencer a little bit, and I'm aware that when she needs to, she *can* find courage and self-belief – it's one of the many things I like about her. But she's also got into the *habit* of behaving in a certain way around things that frighten or unsettle her, as we all do, and on this occasion, it didn't serve her *at all!*

As a side note, she did eventually manage to stay still long enough to get her ears pierced, gasping with shock at how straightforward the procedure was once she'd stopped thrashing about in anticipation of pain that never came.

Just What We Do

We all have habits and that's a good thing. In fact, habits are vital because without them we'd have to think about every single thing we need to do in our lives; we'd be learning how to brush our teeth every day and falling down when we tried to walk. But because habits are things we do every minute of every day – even the thoughts that pop into our head are habits – we need to be sure that they're helpful to us, that they serve us.

How do we do this? Well, we take a long, hard look at them and have a good clear out. Just as we'd do with an over-full drawer –

like the one in your kitchen that's stuffed with weird and wonderful things that you're holding on to 'just in case'.

Your head and your actions are pretty much the same. You're hanging on to old habits in the same way you're holding on to that favourite T-shirt in your wardrobe: the one you know doesn't really do the job any longer because there are holes at the sides and a suspicious stain down the front that may or may not be spaghetti. But y'know, you like it!

To put it another way: habits are 'just what you do!' They can be anything from saying yes to things you don't want to do because you're frightened of upsetting someone, to saying no to trying something new or potentially uncomfortable because you're afraid you'll be bad at it or look stupid. But habits can change – *you* can change.

Why Does the Brain Form Habits?

So, why do we have habits in the first place? Besides liberating us from the need to think about every tiny action we do each day, having habits frees us up to learn other things – from a new job to playing the trombone, it really doesn't matter. As life and business coach Pete Cohen, a friend of mine, puts it: Nuns wear habits. We *wear* our habits – until we change out of them. And the way to do that is to change our *perspective* on them.

Our brain doesn't know whether a habit is good or bad – we just do the things we do because we're used to doing them. And that's what makes habits so damn hard to change – we're *so* used to them!

I recently interviewed the neuroscientist Dr Gabija Toleikyte, author of the book *Why The F*ck Can't I Change?* (you can see why that title grabbed my attention). Her insights into the reasons why we behave the way we do are fascinating. We discussed why it is that changing the aspects of our behaviour that don't serve us is something we consistently *want* to do but consistently *fail* to do.

The best way to understand why we find this so difficult is to be aware that our brain is only partly human, yet we try to apply human wishful thinking to our behaviour. Only partly human? Yup. Our brain consists of three main areas: lizard brain, mammal brain and human brain, each of which has a different agenda.

◆ The lizard brain only cares about our physical survival.

◆ The mammal brain wants to keep us safe via the repetition of the same old habits we're used to.

◆ The human brain is the only area that's capable of creating a deliberate change and resisting the temptation to fall back into old habits.

Change Takes Time

It takes courage, love and compassion to change our habits, and these aren't things that we always have to hand. Trying to change our mindset using willpower alone is *never* going to work, no matter how hard we try, or how much we want it to. Why?

Because as soon as it all gets too much, or we become tired or stressed out (which, let's be fair, can happen quite often), we make stupid decisions.

But here's the great part – it's not our fault. It's because different brain areas need different amounts of energy and recovery time, with the lizard brain being the most efficient and the human brain being the costliest.

When we're tired or stressed, we don't have enough energy for the smartest areas of the brain, so we revert to the mammal brain, which is driven by old habits. It's why we reach for the crisps or say things that may cause arguments, even though logically we know better. When we're in that state, we're unable to change, or to give the most empowered responses.

According to Dr Toleikyte, to create a lasting change in our behaviour, we need to manage the energy levels of our different brain areas, do mammal brain-soothing activities and replenish our human brain area. This means that we also need to do small things consistently, rather than frightening our mammal brain by trying to make big changes all at once.

So, instead of thinking, *I'll join a gym and go every single day, and stop eating takeaways, and stop smoking, all in one go!* we need to take small but constructive steps towards getting what we want, cutting out one thing, or taking on one new challenge. If you decide to do it all at once, I guarantee that you'll find it too hard and you'll have given up before the week's out. That doesn't mean you're weak – it means you tried to do too much in one go.

The same logic works for disagreements, whether with someone else or with yourself: 'I want crisps. No, you don't, you're just bored! *Oh, my God – shut up!*' It takes us 15 minutes to calm down once we get fired up, so Dr Toleikyte recommends always walking away from a disagreement (or if it's with yourself, walking away from the crisp cupboard), cooling down and then coming back to it. This has been scientifically proven (by neuroscientists, who know their stuff) to be the only way to keep thinking rationally.

What Are Your Habits?

Think about the things you do that are a habit: the things you do without thinking. For me, it's brushing my teeth – I don't give it much thought, mainly because I do it at the start of the day when I'm tired and at the end of the day when I want to go to bed.

Have you ever tried to brush your teeth with your 'other' hand? It's so hard and it feels so strange! That's what introducing a new habit is like, and that's why you give up. Not because you're weak and have no willpower but because your brain's saying: *Stop! What are you doing? That's not how we do things!*

It's exactly the same with our emotional habits and behaviour patterns. You may be in the habit of lashing out if someone says something hurtful to you, because you've been hurt before. Or in the habit of not speaking up because you're afraid you may be called bossy or demanding, or because your family didn't encourage it, so you've never broken the habit of staying quiet.

Just because it's something you've always done, doesn't mean it's something you need to continue doing. Once you get your head around this it's so much easier to cut yourself some slack for not being able to stick to changes in your behaviour.

Journal Time ✍

Have a think about your daily habits and then in your journal, list them under the following headings:

♦ Food

♦ Exercise

♦ Sleep

♦ Attitude

♦ Relationships with loved ones

♦ Relationships with friends

♦ How you spend your free time

♦ Where your mind automatically wanders to when you have a free moment

Ask yourself: *Why do I have these habits?* Are these things 'just what you do' or have you *trained* yourself to do them because you've done them so often, they're familiar to you? For example, picking up your phone to check Facebook or Instagram while the kettle boils, while you eat, as you watch TV, when you go to the bathroom, when your children are talking to you. If you're old enough to remember life before mobile phones, what did you do? It sounds strange kids, but guess what? We used to stare into space, think about stuff, look at the other people in the queue, stare up at the sky, look our children in the face.... Pretty radical, eh?

Becoming Aware of Our Habitual Response

To change our habits and our patterns of behaviour, the first thing we need to do is believe that we *can* change them. Sometimes this fear of change comes from a natural wariness of the unknown; after all, who are you if you're not the person who does this thing? But very often we aren't even aware that we have emotional habits that aren't serving us.

I have a friend whose automatic response to anything is: 'Oh no, I couldn't possibly do that. I'm not smart enough.' Or 'Oh no, I'd never be brave enough to try that.' Or 'Oh no, I'd make a right mess of that – you go ahead, that's not for me.' She says these things so naturally, without considering whether she's capable of doing the thing that's been mentioned, or even if she wants to do it. Her habitual response is that she cannot.

I gently pointed this out to her recently and we ended up having an interesting conversation about it. She genuinely hadn't given any thought to her response; it was simply what she always said – it was a habit.

I asked my friend why she believed she did this. After a moment's consideration she said, 'It's just what I've always done.' I gently dug a little deeper and eventually she revealed that her habit of thinking this way about herself had started when she was young. While she was growing up, her mother had been very strict with her, and as a result she became nervous and hesitant, which in turn made her clumsy. This irritated her mum: 'You're so clumsy!' was a phrase that rang out often in their home.

This transferred to my friend telling herself that she was clumsy (which she isn't – no more than anyone else) and also that she was stupid and unable to express herself properly.

I told her that this isn't how I perceive her at all; I see a very capable woman who runs her own small business from home and is artistic and creative. She's a wonderfully kind and patient mother and has a warm, loving relationship with her husband that many people would do *anything* to have! She was taken aback because she'd never thought of herself in this light before: it was not her *habit* to do so.

Teaching Ourselves New Habits

The way we feel about ourselves may not seem like a habit that we're capable of breaking, but it very much is. Think about what you tell yourself when you look in the mirror, and when you're feeling stressed or overwhelmed.

Or even how you interact with strangers. Do you automatically look down or away? Or do you meet their eyes and smile, maybe even ask how they are? Frown and look down and you'll be met with the same negative emotional response. But smile and there's a chance that the world will smile with you.

One of the things I regularly used to say to myself, or to anyone who asked me to do more than one thing at a time, was: 'Oh, I can't multitask. I'm useless at it.' Then one day I thought about what I did as a job. For a quarter of a century, I was a live TV host. This is a specific skill because you have to get it right every time – there are no retakes and people are watching. It might not sound like much but that's because you're used to seeing people who are very good at it – trust me, if you ever saw someone who couldn't do it, you'd know!

Hosting a live TV show means reading a script of scrolling words while simultaneously listening to someone talk in your ear about something totally different. Without missing a word, without getting sidetracked, and while taking on board both streams of information.

Doing this in front of a live studio audience, as well as panellists and guests, adds another dimension of concentration because you're aware that you're being watched not only by the audience at home, who only see your face and will notice any twitching of the eyebrows, but also by the studio audience and the guest sitting next to you, who's counting on *you* to keep them relaxed and calm.

It's a lot like patting your head, rubbing your tummy, hopping on one leg and reciting a poem while trying to remember items moving past you on a conveyor belt. All while smiling and holding in your tummy, because all that anyone at home will notice is whether you stumbled or if your dress doesn't suit you.

I did this for years and was very good at it. I was known as a 'safe pair of hands' in the industry; the one who could stay calm in a crisis (and there are always crises happening behind the scenes!); the one who could handle difficult people and situations with grace and ease.

Yet at home, until I started running my business with my husband and had to train myself to focus on that, I'd start and never finish a hundred things a day. I was so used to multitasking in just one specific way in my job that I felt I was useless at it anywhere else.

Our habits may be the cause of our lack of self-belief, simply because we've allowed them to define us.

I came to realize, however, that I wasn't permanently bad at this thing – I just wasn't in the habit of working in a different way, and I needed to stop telling myself that I couldn't do it. I needed to break that pattern of self-talk because it wasn't doing me any good at all while trying to navigate running a business. I had to teach myself how to do this thing. I needed to work through the discomfort of trying something new until it became a habit.

And then I realized that what I do isn't multitasking at all, in the sense of doing many things at once. I simply needed to learn the skill of moving from one thing to another repeatedly until everything's complete. That was the bit I struggled with – I was so used to doing everything at once, like a busy cartoon octopus, that leaving something unfinished and remembering to come back to it again was impossible.

Well, it was impossible until it became possible – and that's the point. I formed new habits in my brain. I learned to work with a daily planner – something I'd never had to do before. I wrote down what I needed to get done every week and then broke that down into daily tasks, then hourly tasks. Anything that didn't get finished was carried over to the next day, or the following week – and that was okay.

In fact, it was to be expected, as it's rare that any job gets completed in the timeframe expected of it. This was a revelation to me; I was used to working on a live TV show where if it didn't go to time, we'd crash off air!

After months of extreme discomfort and fumbling my way around in the dark, I made new habits for myself, and today, working in this way feels natural to me. I've also stopped the habit of telling myself I can't do something; I just don't know how to do it *yet*.

Keep Trying

Life coach Pete Cohen says that the first 10 times we try to do something new it's *unbearable*. Then it becomes *uncomfortable*.

And if we keep doing it, we become *unstoppable*. This is what we need to keep reminding ourselves: it's hard to do new things, but it's not impossible.

The ancient Greek philosopher Aristotle said, 'We are what we repeatedly do.' And that applies whether it's a helpful thing that we do or an unhelpful one. You don't wake up one morning able to speak a foreign language fluently or play the piano – you become good at these things by practising them regularly.

In the same way, you don't wake up one morning 10 pounds overweight and feeling sluggish, wondering how the hell *that* happened. You might think it, but it's been building all along – you just haven't been paying attention.

'Excellence, then, is not an act, but a habit.' This was Aristotle again, speaking in the 4th century BCE, which illustrates that we humans have been wrestling with the desire to change our habits for the better for thousands of years.

If you want to install the habits of success, or the habit of being brave enough to go for things that seem completely out of your reach, you won't do so by performing one super-brave thing and then calling it quits. It's about doing things that don't seem sexy or brave at all. They may even be painful things that don't bring any immediate rewards or satisfaction. But when you do those things for an extended period, *that's* when the incredible things happen.

Making Courage a Habit

A few years ago, I took part in a TV show called *Tumble*, in which a group of people with no previous experience of gymnastics were trained to perform complex routines live on TV; the contestants were partnered up with professionals who showed them the ropes.

The training was *brutal*. It involved five hours of training a day, five days a week. The warm-up alone took an hour and was tougher than any exercise class you can imagine. HIIT, Blaze, Spin – these have nothing on what we were expected to do! Pull-ups, push-ups, burpees, hanging off bars, being pushed into the splits, handstands, back bends, flips, spinning on a hoop suspended in the air. For hours and hours on end, all I'd hear from the trainer was: 'Again. Again. Again.'

In the two months of training before the show, I badly sprained both ankles, ripped the skin off my hands and behind my knees, and fainted from over-exertion. Every day I'd drive home from training, limp into the house and pour myself a cold bath, topping it up with bags of ice. I'd lower myself in slowly and force myself to sit there for at least 15 minutes to help the swelling in my bruised body go down. And then I'd get up the next day and do it all over again.

On the first night of the live TV show, I had an accident during the dress rehearsal. My partner and I were coming to the end of our routine – where I was holding on to him, suspended upside down from a hoop dangled from the ceiling of the huge studio – when our hands slipped.

The muscles in my shoulder tore, and I fell from what felt like the sky onto the crash mat below. The breath was knocked out of me, and I saw stars – and not only the concerned faces of the other contestants. I was checked over by paramedics before being carried out of the studio to see the physio, who taped my shoulder back into place. I was given painkillers and then taken to make-up to get ready for the show.

That night, millions of people watched from home as I sashayed onto the studio floor, flung my leg over an aerial hoop and grinned as I was whisked into the air. I spun and twirled, smiling broadly as I pulled myself into the same position which hours earlier had seen me fall through the air.

I barely heard the crowd over the noise of my thudding heart, and adrenaline kept the pain in my shoulder at bay. Every one of the pull-ups, push-ups, sprints, flips and ice-cold baths I'd done in training gave me the mental and physical strength I needed to perform, pushing me through my very real fear of falling, of pain, of looking stupid in front of millions of viewers.

Every one of those painful, repetitive things I'd done in the months beforehand had become part of me, ingrained in me, so I was able to do what needed to be done – despite the fear.

When we think of courage in action, we often think of soldiers or an elite force like the SAS. The everyday life of a soldier is spent training for the things they need to be good at, day in, day out, until they're used to the pressure that being brave requires. They're able to keep a cool head because their habits kick in.

So, in the very same way as excellence, courage too becomes a habit, because learning how to repeatedly face the things that scare and intimidate us means that they no longer frighten us – they're just an obstacle to overcome, like any other.

Defying Our Internal Opposition

Gymnastics and elite forces may seem like odd bedfellows but having dipped my toe into both worlds through my participation in the TV shows *Tumble* and *SAS: Who Dares Wins*, I can tell you that the thought process behind them is the same.

By repeatedly doing uncomfortable, difficult things that cause suffering – where you must tell yourself to keep going when every part of you wants to stop, to quit, to do something easier instead because you don't think you can take any more – you learn to work through your own internal opposition.

By repeatedly doing difficult things, you learn to shut down the voice inside that says you can't, that you're afraid, that you'll get it wrong.

And once you get used to doing this – once this becomes your new habit of behaviour – facing down any *external* opposition to whatever it is you dream of achieving becomes so much easier. Because *you've unlocked your courage, reclaimed your power and learned to believe in yourself.*

You'll always have opposition. It could be external opposition from people who don't want you to change, but the biggest opposition you'll face is the opposition inside you. The voice that says: *There's no point in doing this. You've tried it before, and it didn't work.*

You'll *always* have that voice in your head. However, it's not as loud when you're in flow – when you've simply *got* to do something because you love it and you're inspired by it. Then the voice becomes less scratchy, and quieter. And that takes practice.

Like learning to brush your teeth with your other hand, like asking yourself why you automatically say, 'Oh, I couldn't possibly do that', it *always* feels strange and difficult when you first start doing something new. But just because something's difficult to do, it doesn't mean it's impossible to do. It just means you aren't in the habit of doing it, so you don't believe that you can. *But you can.*

The Habits of Success

When we're feeling stuck, afraid and angry with the world, it seems like those who are succeeding in life appear to know something that we don't. It's as if they've been given an insider's tip on what to do.

But if you take the time to read about the lives of successful people – for example, those who've done something remarkable in sport, business or entertainment – you'll find that their success has come about through a mixture of hard work, smart work and dedication.

Of course, luck comes into it, too. There may be times when it feels like no matter what you do, the breaks won't come. It gets harder and harder, and you simply can't try any more. That's okay. We've all got to that point and sometimes stopping, stepping back and walking away is absolutely the right thing to do. But when you dig into the habits of highly successful people, that insider's tip is always dedication and hard work.

Now, before you get all riled up, I'm not saying that you don't work as hard as they do. Not at all. I'm saying that they work smarter and they're more dedicated. They stand back and look at what they're working on, figure out whether what they're doing day in, day out is taking them closer to their goal, adjust their route and keep going.

They're in the habit of working *on themselves and what they're doing*, not just working in general. And they keep doing it. There's no secret that you haven't been told and they have – it's all about habits.

**A habit that every successful person has
– one that sets them apart from others
– is a desire to keep learning.**

This may seem obvious when you're just starting out: of course, you'll want to learn all that you can. But being in the habit of continually opening our minds to new thought processes and new ideas is the only way we can break away from patterns of behaviour that are keeping us stuck in the same place.

Try spending 15 minutes a day learning something new. You might insist that you don't have a second spare to think straight, let alone learn something new, but you do: 15 minutes is literally 1 per cent of your day.

You could listen to an interesting podcast on your journey to work or on the way back from the school run, or while walking the dog – whatever. You can do it whenever you want to but do try to fit it into your day. I listen to podcasts or audio books while I'm doing my make-up and drying my hair, or while I'm making dinner (I put my headphones in and crack on).

I also subscribe to an app called Headway that condenses non-fiction books into 15-minute summaries. It's a great way to dip into informative books before making the time commitment to dive all in. I always hear something that I'd never have known otherwise.

Breaking the Habit of Giving Up

One of the best habits you can install is doing what you say you're going to do. Because the brain remembers every time. Think about it – if you give up every time you start something new because you've found it too difficult (and remember, it will always be difficult, simply because it's new), your brain will remember this and prepare you for giving up in the future.

It'll send you little reminders as well: 'Remember that time you tried to learn Spanish and it was really hard? And how good it felt when you gave up and didn't have to feel stupid for not remembering all those words or didn't have time to do the homework and your tutor gave you that "look"? Just do that again because it was so much easier!'

Giving up simply feeds into our sense of failure, of fear, and it reinforces our lack of self-belief.

Because why should we believe in ourselves if we're the flaky friend who always cancels and stops trying? There's a way to break that habit of giving up, of simply reverting to that unhelpful pattern of behaviour. And that's by reminding yourself of a time in the past when you *stuck at something* and saw it through.

Journal Time ✑

Asking yourself the following questions and responding to them in your journal will remind your brain that you have *experience* of doing difficult things; it will stop it from automatically reminding you how much easier it is to simply give up.

The trick here is to give your brain a memory of a time when you *succeeded* at something, so that it will hang on to that feeling of satisfaction, that glow of pride and sense of achievement, that buzz of pure excitement when you completed it. So, as you're doing this exercise, try to *connect emotionally* with the experience of sticking with something – really *feel* it.

1. Think of a time when you set out to learn something new:

    –   How difficult was it when you started to learn it?

    –   How did you overcome that difficulty?

    –   What made you stick with it?

2. Really *relive* the experience:

    –   How did it feel when it was difficult?

    –   Where did you get your strength from?

    –   How did you make yourself *believe* you could do it?

    –   What was it that made you keep going?

    –   How did it feel when you managed to achieve what you'd set out to do?

    –   How *excited* were you? I bet you couldn't wait to tell everyone what you'd done!

Why am I asking you these questions? Because 99.999 per cent of the time when we try to do something – whether it's attempting something new or giving something up – we rely solely on willpower to get it done. But as I mentioned earlier, willpower alone simply doesn't work because it relies on us feeling like doing something or having the *will* to do it.

You need to be able to do these things, and to break your previous behaviour patterns, even when you *don't want to*. And the only way to do that is to attach a positive emotion to it – something that will trigger a good feeling every time you think of it. Therefore, replaying a time in your life when you did something you were proud of, writing down what it was and how you overcame it and really digging into what made you stick at it, even when it was tough – all these things will help trigger you in a positive way to break your habits and behaviour patterns.

A Mental Blueprint for Success

So, how can you take all those feelings and experiences and use them with an issue you're facing *now*? Well, as you reminded yourself (and your brain) in the previous exercise, you've already succeeded at learning or trying something difficult, so just think how wonderful it will feel to do it again!

The thing you want to do now can be anything at all, simple or complex: from going to bed earlier so you get seven hours' solid sleep a night to exercising every day and eating foods that nourish your body; from stopping smoking to meditating for 10 minutes every day for a week to calm your whirling mind; or leaving a job or a relationship and having the courage to start new ones.

Journal Time ✍

Grab your journal and do the following:

1. Visualize yourself already doing that thing you want to do – let yourself really wallow in this image, roll around in it.

2. Write down how you feel, now that you've broken the habit, the old behaviour pattern, that you wanted to change.

3. Let your brain absorb all these positive emotions associated with changing that habit or behaviour. How happy you feel for overcoming this challenge! What a sense of achievement you feel for doing something that was hard! How pleased with yourself you are for keeping going even when you didn't want to! How proud you are for *believing* you could do it!

You're setting yourself a mental blueprint for success simply by doing this exercise. The more you do it, the more you'll feel how *amazing* it is to break the behaviour patterns that are holding you back, and the quicker your brain will recall these positive emotions and help you keep going, even when you don't want to.

Don't let fear or hardship get in your way of feeling this great. Remember: you've done hard things before, and you can do them again.

Recognize that the habits that got you into the situation you're in now will *never* be the habits that get you out of it. That's just logic, so don't be scared of it. Be excited by it! You're going to change things, and your life is going to be better – how great is that?

Your Change Your Habits Challenge

Coming up is a tried-and-tested questioning technique that I know will help you break your habits. First, I'll give you an example of how it was used on me by Liam James Collins at The Coaching Masters during my training to become an accredited life coach. It blew my mind. The habit that I wanted to break was eating platefuls of the delicious cookies my 14-year-old daughter was baking.

Liam: What needs to change within your environment to make this change?

Me: I just need to stay out of the kitchen while she's baking the cookies because they smell so good!

Liam: What behaviour do you need to adopt to make this change?

Me: I need to not eat them – to say no.

Liam: What skills do you have, or need to obtain, in order to make this change?

Me: I need more willpower.

Liam: Why is this change important to you?

Me: Apart from the obvious weight gain issue, eating the cookies makes me feel sick; I have a reaction to the amount of sugar and dairy in them. Even though they taste delicious, and I could devour a whole batch of them, I'm sick for days afterwards.

Liam: What assumptions are you making about this change?

Me: That my daughter will think I don't love her because I won't eat the cookies that she's baked for us to enjoy while we sit together and watch our weekly mum/daughter movie.

Liam: Who do you need to become in order to make this change?

Me: Someone strong and loving who my daughter knows is a good example of a loving woman.

Liam: How will you be remembered if you make this change?

Me: As someone who showed her daughter that love doesn't mean saying yes to things that make you sick or hurt you. Love means explaining that what the other person is doing is unintentionally hurting you and finding a way that makes you both feel happy.

I thought I was going to learn how to say no to cookies, but instead I found I was teaching my daughter that love means accepting things that hurt you. Like I said, my mind was blown!

I learned that the strong me is someone who doesn't touch anything that hurts her and who leads by loving example. I imagined this new persona as a Beyoncé-esque woman called Sasha (as in Sasha Fierce) who looks smokin' hot in denim shorts and always has a wind machine nearby. Sasha wouldn't even consider eating those cookies! But she would have found an even better way for her and her daughter to show each other their love – one that most likely came with an arms-in-the-air chorus.

You see what I'm getting at? I replaced one belief for another, and this one was stronger and more vibrant, and it pulled me away from any limiting beliefs I may have had around those cookies.

Journal Time ✑

Now it's your turn. Think about what you'd like to change about yourself or your life. Don't go too crazy by listing 10 or more things – you'll only become overwhelmed and give up. I'm not throwing you shade, it's just the truth. So, really think about the *one thing* that you'd like to change right now. Write it down in your journal and then ask yourself these questions:

♦ What needs to change within my environment to make the change that I want to make?

♦ What behaviour do I need to adopt to make this change?

♦ What skills do I have, or need to obtain, in order to make this change?

♦ Why is this change important to me?

♦ What assumptions am I making about this change?

♦ Who do I need to become to make this change?

♦ How will I be remembered if I make this change?

Remember: everything that we do is done out of habit. From the moment we wake up in the morning until we go to bed at night, we perform little habits and patterns that have become so much a part of us that we don't even notice them any more.

Get excited about changing your habits and patterns. Remember that making these changes to your life is within your control and it has been all along. You just need to *believe* that you have the ability to change and make *that* your daily habit.

In the next chapter, we're going to look at how the little things you do at the start and end of each day have the power to change your life. Which means that by the end of tomorrow, you'll have already put processes in place that will take you in a whole new direction. I can't *wait* to show you how!

Rework Your Daily Routines

'Let today be the day you give up who you've been for who you can become.'

HAL ELROD

Yesterday we spoke about our habits and about how the things that we do every single day add up to the person we are. Today we're going to have a look at making positive habits part of our morning and evening routines.

You might be wondering what this has to do with believing in yourself and unlocking your courage, but you'll soon discover that it has *everything* to do with it. As I mentioned yesterday, our brain likes to do what it understands are the simplest, most effective things for us to survive. It makes them into habits so that we don't have to think about them too much – so we can get on with the important stuff like staying alive.

Our daily routines are intricately entwined with this because they're the behavioural patterns that help us function the most efficiently. You might not think that you have a morning or evening routine, but you do. We all have daily routines, and they affect every part of our everyday life.

The way our day begins tends to be a marker for how it continues, and this has a huge impact on what we believe about ourselves and how we face the outside world. I know that if I wake up feeling exhausted because I watched too many episodes of *Schitt's Creek* on Netflix the previous evening and lost a couple of hours of valuable sleep, I'm not going to be in the greatest of moods.

Waking up grumpy means that I'm not in the best mindset to make good choices from the start, so there's a pretty good chance that I *won't* want to exercise and that I *will* eat sugar, carbs and coffee for breakfast, lunch and dinner. This makes me jittery, overreactive and oversensitive to everything, and by the evening I'm feeling even worse.

It's not pretty seeing all of that written down, but it's the ugly truth! Not that I'm blaming *Schitt's Creek* or *Ted Lasso* or whatever show I happen to be enthralled with at the time: I just need to have the willpower to switch off the damn TV and go to bed – the show will still be there for me the following night.

Start and End Each Day with Intention

If this has made you raise a weary hand in recognition, you'll know that you certainly won't be feeling courageous enough to try anything challenging or new when your body and brain are exhausted from just getting through the day: they don't have the capacity to fit in anything else.

So, when you do try something challenging or new, it's going to be a million times harder for you than if you'd tried it from a place of being rested, well-fed and energized. That's simple logic. No wonder you don't believe that you can do anything or are afraid of trying something away from your norm – you've been doing the equivalent of attempting a 100-metre sprint blindfolded with your legs tied together. It's not surprising that you fell over!

Journal Time ✍

Ask yourself the following questions:

1. What's your daily routine?

Pause here for a moment and visualize your day from start to finish. What do you do from the minute you open your eyes until the moment you crawl back into bed again? You'll soon see that there are little things you do every single day without fail. Write them all down in your journal.

2. Do these things serve me?

If your first action when you wake up is to reach for your phone and start scrolling through Instagram to see what everyone else is doing, I'd say 100 per cent no: this doesn't serve you. You're already comparing your day with those of people who aren't really a part of your life.

You may think that considering your daily routine is irrelevant to you because the things in your life that are causing stress or discomfort are beyond your control. And to a certain extent you're right: many of the things which happen to us *are* out of our control. But what *is* in our control is the way we *react* to them. And the way we react begins with the mindset we have when they happen.

Little Things Matter

How do we keep a calm, grounded mindset? We make it a habit – by starting and finishing each day with the intention of getting the very best out of it. This idea isn't new – it's how great men and women have always dealt with the difficult situations that life has continued to throw at them. Because that's one thing we can definitely count on – life will always throw hard stuff our way.

In a speech he gave at the University of Texas in 2014, Naval Admiral William H. McRaven, ninth commander of the United States Special Operations Command, told the assembled students about the training he received when he became a US Navy SEAL.[1] His words, beautifully and eloquently spoken, went viral because of their power and simplicity. If you have a moment, watch the recording on YouTube.

Admiral McRaven said many inspiring things about the power of one person to change the world, but today I'm going to focus on his thoughts regarding the importance of a morning routine. In a nutshell, this is what he said on the subject:

'Every morning, we were required to make our bed to perfection... [and] the wisdom of this simple act has been proven to me many times over. If you make your bed every morning, you will have accomplished your first task of the day... and it will encourage you to do another task, and another, and another. By the end of the day, that one task completed will have turned into many tasks completed.

'Making your bed will also reinforce the fact that little things in life matter. If you can't do the little things right, you will never do the big things right. And, if by chance you have a miserable day, you will come home to a bed that is made – that you made – and a made bed gives you encouragement that tomorrow will be better.'

BOOM! 'A made bed gives you encouragement that tomorrow will be better.' That's everything you need in 11 words.

Why? Because of what that bed *symbolizes*. Some days will be terrible and every single thing that you try will go wrong. People will hurt you, desert you and let you down. Things will fail. Disasters come into our life that split us in two with pain.

But without the hope that things will be better tomorrow, how do we find the courage to carry on? Believing in a better day doesn't come from nowhere – it comes from the systems we put in place. It's the scaffolding we build within ourselves that creates the courage we need to keep going.

Living a life of courage and conviction begins and ends with the little things; as Admiral McRaven says, if we can't do the little things right, then we'll never be able to do the big things right. Often when we come up against difficult situations, we're looking at them from the perspective of someone who hasn't mastered doing the little things, not knowing that every one of those little things builds a resilience inside us. A muscle memory kicks into action when needed because it knows how to handle it.

When I heard this incredible speech, I already had a morning routine, and interestingly, I'd instinctively done the things that Admiral McRaven spoke about. Making my bed makes me feel good; it's a calming and structured way to start my day.

I pull the bottom sheet tight and fluff up my cover and pillows so they're plump and ready for me. I lay out my cushions and I smooth down the extra blanket, and then I stand back and admire my work. I've made that beautiful bed, and I start the day feeling good.

And each night, whether my day has gone well or to hell, I climb into a beautifully made bed, which makes everything better. I *deserve* to get into a beautiful, well-made bed after a long day! I *deserve* the encouragement that things will be better tomorrow! And so do you.

It's All about Balance

Have a think about how you want to start and end your day. How can you exchange the things you're doing now that don't serve you for things that do? Breaking a habit isn't about simply stopping what you're doing – it's about replacing it with something else, so that you form new habits.

Simply stopping something will leave a space, and as science will tell you, nature always fills a void. So, trying to stop doing one thing without replacing it with something else is impossible – you need to replace the unhelpful thing you've been doing with something helpful.

Pay attention to how you define your habits – they're not 'right' or 'wrong', they're simply 'helpful' or 'unhelpful'.

It's much easier to put aside a habit that our brain recognizes as a neutral thing that's unhelpful to us, than beat ourselves up for doing something we see as 'wrong'.

Our daily routines don't have to be punishing to get results – I genuinely think that this is a myth we've bought into because most of the books and articles written about the routines of successful people are about men. There's nothing wrong with that – I'm fascinated by anyone's journey – but to me this only tells part of the story.

There are many ways to have a routine that serves us, that's helpful and which doesn't involve punishment. Routines will always involve discomfort – that's a given because any kind of growth or change means discomfort – but punishment is an altogether different thing. It's one-upmanship of the most ridiculous kind.

Sometimes it helps to call a routine a 'ritual' because the latter is something we see as a blessing to ourselves. I imagine a ritual as something gentle, something done with love. I try to see it as doing something to show myself love.

No Need to Push

Look up the words 'morning routine' online and your results will be bulging with articles about successful people who get up at 4 a.m., hit the gym and are in the office before the rest of their team have even hit snooze, smashing their way through the day with a schedule that'd make your head spin.

Now, I *love* being successful and filling my day with good stuff, but living this way is *exhausting*. I know it is because I used to live like this. To be honest, it's also not sustainable, not at that extreme level of exertion.

As some of you may know if you've read my last book, *This Girl Is On Fire*, at one time I was up and in the gym every day before work, pounding the treadmill and lifting weights before my colleagues had even opened their eyes. I did this while listening to motivational podcasts telling me to push harder, work longer, keep going. And I did... until I burned out and fell down.

That was three years ago and although I still do some form of exercise every day, I don't push myself to be the best at it, like I used to. I've started running again after a long hiatus. It was painful and horribly slow at first, and I spent a lot of time chastising myself for letting my fitness slip, for feeling sluggish, for the weight I'd gained and the momentum I'd lost.

And then I had to take myself to one side and give myself a stern talking to. I'd forgotten to put *context* into this situation. My momentum had been perfectly good (if not great), thank you very much, but it had just been in a different direction. Like the rest of the human race, I'd been living through an unprecedented global pandemic. I'd also quit my job and started a new business and was working every hour to keep our family afloat.

The fact that I hadn't done the same amount of exercise as I used to was hardly a surprise – and by the way, wasn't I still doing yoga every morning and walking 2–3 miles a day? *Shut up woman!*

Having learned my lesson from pushing myself so hard that I burned out, I now make sure that my daily routines are those that serve every part of me, not just those that are geared towards smashing the hell out of every goal, be it fitness, work or otherwise.

It doesn't mean that I don't want to succeed in those things – I absolutely do want to be the best in everything I do! But I understand now that there must be a balance in all things or else, you've guessed it, we wobble and fall over.

Your Daily Routine Challenge

Success in anything we try to do – and that includes finding the courage in our heart to believe in ourselves again – comes through doing small things consistently, not just by smashing things up to get to the next level. Yes, at times that's also needed, but not every time.

Maybe this is a female perspective, but I like to think of it as being likewater. Water is fluid and clear, and rather than wasting its energy trying to smash through a rock it will find the smoothest path around it, using little force yet still continuing on its way. But over time, that same water can find its way through the toughest stone, smoothing it down bit by bit, using the same consistent level of energy.

Perhaps it serves you best to think of forming a routine, or ritual, that works for you in this way. Rather than being put off by the idea of smashing that lock on your inner courage, you can consistently work on it until it frees itself, joyfully unleashing the self-belief within.

Let's take a look at the things you can do to build up your intention to have a great day, every day – to live each day with the courage to do things that serve you and the self-belief to know that you're capable of being the person you want to be. You've considered the things that you're doing currently and have seen what isn't serving you, what isn't helpful. So, what follows is a morning and evening routine that you can use as a framework to build your own. These are the things that work for me, and I've put my own twist on them based on my learnings and observations of others.

If your own morning and evening routines are to work, they need to fit in with your lifestyle – with your family and your working life. The key is to do something consistently that works for you. Don't try and do everything described below in exactly the order shown – instead, use my suggestions as a guide and establish your own routines. The only thing that I'd challenge you to stick to is ensuring your routines have enough grit in them to push you forwards.

Your Morning Routine

◆ **As you wake up, try to recall what you were dreaming about.**
   Keep your eyes closed and go over it in your head. What do you think your dream was trying to tell you? Was it letting you know what it is you're *really* afraid of? Was it reassuring you

that everything's going to be okay if you just let go? Grab your journal and jot down your thoughts before you forget them.

♦ **Immediately after getting up, make your bed.** Properly. Smooth the under sheet, shake out the duvet, plump up the pillows, pull everything straight and tight. How great does that look? You've already achieved something, and you've only been up for one minute! And the best part is, you'll have a wonderful treat waiting for you later – who doesn't *love* getting into a beautifully made bed at the end of the day? You deserve it!

♦ **Drink a large glass of water to rehydrate your body.** I like to prepare mine the night before with a slice of lemon and then leave it next to the bed, so I don't have to fiddle about getting one from the kitchen. It helps flush out toxins in your system, meaning you've already done something great without any effort at all.

♦ **Move your body.** You don't have to kick the hell out of every day by smashing it at the gym, but you need to move your body, even if it's simply to properly stretch. I do yoga most mornings, and it's part of my routine to pull on the stretchy leggings and top, brush my teeth and then make my way downstairs and onto the yoga mat before I'm even fully awake.

Do I enjoy it every morning? No. Am I glad I did it after every session? Undoubtedly. To make things easier, I lay out my clothes on the bathroom windowsill the night before, so they're ready for me as soon as I wake up. I sometimes pull them on while I'm sitting on the toilet, eyes barely open. So, by the time I've brushed my teeth and washed my face, still half asleep, suddenly I'm standing in my bathroom ready to go.

♦ **Take a probiotic to kick-start your gut.** Do this at least 10 minutes before you eat anything and let it do its thing while you carry on getting ready. Then you can have your hot drink, your breakfast, or whatever it is you eat to start your day. I take my probiotic before I do my yoga as I don't eat anything until after I've finished anyway. You can try a small glass of kefir, too, or a gut shot, whatever works for you.

♦ **Think about what you're watching or listening to.** How does it make you feel? After exercising, I take my phone into the shower with me (it sits on a shelf that's far away from the water) and I listen to the radio. I used to start the day listening to rolling news and phone-in shows – I did this for years because of my job. But now I listen to a breakfast show that has interesting conversation and great music, so I feel that I'm across everything but still in a bouncy mood. It's made such a difference; I'm not bogged down by every awful thing that's happening in the world after hours of discussion about it.

♦ **End your regular shower with a blast of cold water.** Prepare yourself by getting into the right mental state, which you can do using your breath. Breathe in and out really deeply, sucking the air in through your nose and blowing it out through your mouth, hard. Do this a few times and then step underneath the cold water for as long as you can take it, anywhere from 30 seconds to two minutes is great.

The breathing is so important because this is what will pump your body full of oxygen and get those blood vessels working, invigorating your heart, your lungs and your skin. These are the organs that you want to be in great working order as you go about your day – and you've just given them an amazing start!

I try and last a whole song under the cold water. If it's a song I like, then I really focus on it as I breathe in and out. Sometimes I'll even last for a couple of songs, jigging about in the shower (carefully, obviously, as I've no desire to end up naked and soaking in A&E, which would be so embarrassing). It takes something functional – a morning shower – and turns it into something interesting, invigorating and fun.

♦ **Meditate.** You don't have to spend hours doing it, even five minutes makes a difference. Find what works for you, whether it's an app (try Calm, Headspace or Insight Timer) or just sitting for a few minutes with your eyes closed, counting your breath in and out, up to 10 times. It all helps.

If you can meditate for longer, however, I'd urge you to. I recently heard the former monk Jay Shetty, author of the book *Think Like a Monk*, use a great analogy.[2] He said that some people tell him they've tried meditating for five minutes a day and it doesn't do anything for them. He likened this to getting to know someone. If you spent five minutes a day with a person but cut off your contact with them just when it was getting interesting – and you did this same thing daily – you'd find your time with them frustrating. You'd never get any further in your relationship with them.

However, if you put in the time and got to know the person really well, and then went on to marry them and build a life with them, spending that same five minutes of quality time a day would take on a whole different perspective. You'd instinctively know how to tune in to what they needed from you, and those few minutes together could be a really powerful thing.

What I'm getting at is that five minutes of meditation is better than nothing, but if it doesn't seem to be working for you, perhaps it's because you need to spend *more* time on it, rather than simply giving up. See my guide to meditation in Day 6.

Your Evening Routine

This is just as important as your morning routine – in fact, I think that a morning routine always starts the evening before. Not only does it end your day on the right note, helping you to get a good night's sleep, it also makes things easier for you when you first wake up, getting your day off to an amazing start.

◆ **Pick a cut-off time and put down your phone.** If you're watching TV, you don't need your phone by your side. Focus on what you're watching. If you want to check it during the ad breaks, put it on the other side of the room so you have to get up for it.

And don't scroll mindlessly – you've done enough of that today. This is something that drives me absolutely bonkers about my husband. He sits with his phone in his hand all evening, scrolling through social media for hours, watching thousands of golf videos or people doing pull-ups. I have to pause what I'm watching every time he says: 'Oh, my God, look at this putt, babe. Wow, look at this guy doing a pull-up with his little finger.'

I genuinely couldn't give a monkeys about golf swings or how many times a person can haul themselves up and down. I want to watch *Schitt's Creek* in peace and not think about anything other than how awesome Moira Rose is. That's what *I'm* focusing on! So, put down your phone – it's not only better for you as it gives your whirring, dopamine-hunting brain a rest, it'll also stop annoying the person sitting next to you.

♦ **Don't take your phone to your bedroom at night.** Leave it downstairs on charge. This may take a while to get your head around, and you'll have a thousand reasons why not to do this. I was the same. Then I bought a real alarm clock, which removed the 'alarm excuse'. I can live without the sleep apps and everything else; I'm going to bed to sleep, and I know how I feel when I get up – I don't need a device to tell me.

At one time I used sleep apps, but then I found they had the opposite effect on me. I'd wake up feeling great but then the sleep app would tell me I'd had three minutes of quality sleep that night and suddenly I'd feel dreadful. Or I'd think I'd barely slept as I felt so bad, and the app would tell me I'd had eight solid hours. Whaat? So now I just get into bed with enough time to have a good seven hours a night, and that's that. It is what it is.

◆ **Take a glass of water to bed with you.** Not to drink right away but so it's waiting for you in the morning to drink as soon as you get up. If you can pop a slice of fresh lemon in there, even better. I chop a lemon into slices and put them into a glass jar with a sealed lid to keep them fresh and easy to grab when I want one.

◆ **Allow enough time for your nightly routine.** This is the hardest bit for me – I often end up fiddling about with face washing, teeth brushing, flossing, face creams, hand creams, foot creams and any number of other things that I simply 'have' to do. They always take longer than I think, so I allow plenty of time to prevent rushing them before bed. Going to bed in a calm state and feeling that you've done everything you want to is much better for you than watching another episode of something – take it from someone who can lose whole nights in front of a good drama series!

◆ **Check your schedule/the weather and then lay out tomorrow's clothes.** Even better, plan what exercise you're going to do in the morning and lay out your gear the night before. That way you don't waste time thinking about what you might do. The decision is made for you, so all you have to do is get up and do it.

♦ **Put your clothes away or into the laundry basket.** It's much easier to just step out of them and leave them on the floor until the morning, but you've just given yourself another job to do when you wake up – and if you don't feel like doing it now, you sure as hell won't feel like doing it then! You *deserve* to wake up to a clean, tidy bedroom, and it's a much better way to start your day.

Your Nightly Mental Round Off

As you lie in bed with the lights off, ask yourself these four questions. They're very simple and you can spend as much or as little time on them as you like.

1. What am I grateful for today?

2. What am I proud of today?

3. What did I do that took courage today?

4. What am I looking forward to tomorrow?

And as a bonus, I sometimes throw in: What made me smile today?

This is a great thing to do, as it reminds you of something good just before you go to sleep. Some days you'll struggle to list anything, and other days you'll lie in the dark with a big smile on your face thinking of all the wonderful things that happened to you.

Both types of day are equally important. It's vital to take the time to reflect on the moments when things have gone well, to recognize them and sit with them. And on those days when things haven't gone well, it's important to look for the good to be found in them, especially when it feels as if there's none to be found. It's vital to recognize that you have something, no matter how small, to be grateful for, to be proud of.

> **Remind yourself that you did something today that took courage. You did it today. And you'll do it tomorrow. That's how you start to believe it.**

This daily routine challenge may seem like a lot to take on board, so start with one or two routines from the morning and evening list and build up. The point is to find a routine that works for *you*. I promise that within a week, you'll notice a difference in how you feel.

If you still can't motivate yourself to get started, ask yourself: *Why am I not doing these things? Is it because I think they sound difficult, and I don't want to push myself?* If the answer is yes, ask yourself this: *What has difficult got to do with it?* When was not doing something because it looked difficult, or because you may not like it, *ever* a good idea? Especially when that difficult thing is *guaranteed* to help you in some way? Never.

'Not liking it' has *nothing to do with it*. You just need to *believe* it.

***

Now that you've dug into the story you've been telling yourself and the habits you have, and you've looked at reworking your morning and evening routines, in the next chapter we're going to examine the people and voices that you surround yourself with.

You see, you may think that you lack courage because it's just how you are, or because of the thoughts you've had and the things you've been doing, but I'm going to show you that outside forces play a huge part in what we believe to be true about ourselves and our lives. It's going to be a good one – I can't wait to see you tomorrow!

Five to Thrive

'You are the average of the five people you spend the most time with.'

JIM ROHN

Welcome to Day 5 – you're now halfway through! I hope that by now you're starting to see that it's well within your capabilities to make the small but powerful changes you need to unlock the courage and self-belief that you have buried inside you.

Today you're going to learn some life-changing truths about yourself and the reasons why you feel you lack courage and don't believe in yourself. These feelings that you've been holding on to so tightly and have been caged in by haven't come from ideas about yourself that have built up in a vacuum. They've come from the company you surround yourself with. That can be real company, as in your friends, or the company you keep online: the people you follow and what you look at.

So many of us drift into these relationships (either real or online) without giving too much thought as to what they're doing to us. But here's the thing: if you aren't intentional about the people with whom you spend your time, then you may unconsciously be surrounding yourself with those who make you feel small, unworthy or fearful of trying something brave.

We all underestimate the power of the company we keep, and how, bit by bit, every small part of what we do, what we hear, who we surround ourselves with, has a huge part to play in how we see ourselves and whether we stagnate or grow.

This is something we're going examine today – who you surround yourself with, which voices you listen to, what words you read. Just as on the previous days, you may not have given much thought to the idea that the scrolling you do on Facebook, Twitter, Snapchat, TikTok or Instagram, or the coffee and chats you have with your friends, has anything to do with how you feel about yourself and your life. But when you stop to consider it, why wouldn't that be so?

There are 24 hours in every day and if we spend even a few of them listening to the radio, watching TV, reading the news, chatting with friends, looking at what strangers are up to in their lives, it stands to reason that these repeated activities will have an impact on the way we think.

You Are the Company You Keep

'Don't believe everything you read on the internet.'
ABRAHAM LINCOLN

The first time I read that quote I did a double take, and then I doubled over laughing. It sums up everything about where we're at right now – existing in this strange world in which we believe anything that's put in front of us, regardless of its source or authenticity.

We spend hours of our life in this very space, this unregulated part of our existence where anyone can say anything, and we lap it up like thirsty dogs drinking dirty ditch water. We don't even care whether it's good for us or not, or even if it's true. It's there in front of us, to the side of us, behind us, like some strange bad dream that's come to life. Today, the truth is stranger than fiction because we don't even know where the lines are that separate the two.

I don't know if you've watched the documentary-drama *The Social Dilemma* on Netflix, but it's well worth a look. It shows us that even the tech men and women who came up with social media in the first place are now genuinely and seriously concerned about the impact it's having on the world's mental wellbeing.

Social media was created to bring us closer together. Remember when Facebook was just a way to connect with friends you'd lost touch with? Or when Instagram seemed to be a platform where people simply shared pictures of the food they were eating? But social media has since moved on to become a much darker force of subliminal control. How can we know what to believe when it comes to ourselves and our own mindset when we don't know if what's put in front of us on a minute-by-minute basis is fact or fiction?

Even one toxic friend, one social influencer who makes you feel disillusioned, will chip away at your confidence and your self-esteem.

Decades ago, when motivational speaker Jim Rohn spoke about being impacted by the five people you spend the most time with, the world was a simpler place in that you had to be in the same room as someone to be 'spending time with them', although you could perhaps also have a phone call with them.

Of course, you could read a newspaper and switch on the television, but times were very different; people's beliefs, either about themselves or the world that surrounded them, were based on roughly five things, whereas today, we're bombarded by thousands of different influences every moment of the day.

It's a logical assumption that negative people and thoughts hold us back and positive people and thoughts drive us forwards. That's true to an extent, but it's also not as simple as just hanging around with people who tell you that everything's going to be great. That's right up there with thinking that *you just need to believe it* means having a sunny disposition and everything will be okay.

That's not it at all. There's such a thing as 'toxic positivity' – the assumption that no matter how bad or painful a person's situation is, they should be happy and think positive at all times; just plaster on a smile, say nice things and all will be well. I'm sure you know people who are relentlessly positive in this way; I do, and it makes me scratchy being around them.

Your Five to Thrive Challenge

Believing in the power of your abilities, in your mindset and in your courage comes from a place of looking at what you're faced with and knowing that you have the internal tools to deal with it – not simply closing your eyes and hoping for the best.

Many of the so-called 'positive' people in your life may not be as good an influence as they first appear. Where is their positivity based – in truth or in fiction? True positivity is also gritty and real, and it can call you out in order to help you grow.

So, let's get started.

1. Who Do You Follow?

As I've been talking about social media, let's start there. This may already be making you squirm in your seat a little, so let me reassure you – I'm not going to tell you to ditch it all. I love spending time scrolling around, having a little peek at what everyone's up to. It's fun! Of course, it is! Where else are we going to find memes of puppies doing cute things, have a look inside celebrities' beautiful homes or discover people doing amazing things that we'd never normally see because they live on the other side of the world?

Social media is an incredible invention, and it's a part of our lives now. But the thing we seem to forget is that *we're* the ones in control of it. I know that algorithms are at play, and that the very clever people who designed these platforms have ensured that we all get sucked into rabbit holes that take us miles away from where we first started, with a simple click leading to the loss of an hour of our life and filling us up with crazy stuff we didn't need to see.

Yes, those things are happening, and yes, we're all being played by the 'like' button, which has been specifically designed to tap into our primal need to be liked, to feel part of a tribe so we feel valued and safe. All of those things are true. *But you're still in control.*

Despite all the billions of dollars that are thrown into making us go round and round in loops looking at things we don't want to and buying things we don't need to put on display to impress people we'll never meet and never know, you're still in control.

How? Start by looking at the people you follow on social media. Grab your phone now while you're reading this. Launch whichever platform you find yourself on the most and have a little scroll. Look at what everyone's up to. Now ask yourself how you feel while you're looking at them. Be honest. It's only us here, and I won't tell. In fact, I probably feel the same.

Are they pissing you off? Do they make you feel angry, disillusioned, like a failure every time they pop up on your screen? If this is the case, *they're not serving you, so get rid.* Have a clear out, a social media cleanse.

. . . .

Go through your social media accounts and start unfollowing or muting anyone who doesn't make you feel good. It's mind-blowingly liberating!

. . . .

If your instinctive reaction to this is, *Oh, my God. I can't do that!* ask yourself why. If you don't want to upset negative friends by unfollowing them, simply mute them; they won't know you've done it, but it will stop all their negativity flowing out of your phone, into your brain, and telling you that you aren't good enough.

You're more than good enough – you're amazing. You just haven't had the right people telling you so. And you just need to believe it.

You'll feel as if you're taking control of something that's been bothering you for a long time. It's as good as ordering a skip and chucking out a load of crap you no longer need or taking a truck load of clothes you've outgrown to the local charity shop. You'll wonder why you left it so long.

A Word of Caution

Now, you may think that I'm going to tell you to replace those people with positive influences, and up to a point you'd be right. But be very careful with this. There are a lot of people online right now who have cottoned on to the fact that being negative isn't always popular. So, they've reframed what they're doing to give it a veneer of positivity while *still* making you feel bad.

If, for example, the thing that you find difficult to have in your stream is body-related videos or images, then don't start following people who are obsessed with talking about their bodies, even if it's framed in a 'helpful' way. All those videos of people clutching their pert bottoms to show their cellulite isn't going to make you feel good, even though it's dressed up that way and their intentions may be noble and pure. What you'd really be doing is following people who'll fill your feed with pictures of their bottom... and when you say that out loud you can hear how ridiculous it is!

Why do you need to see it? Why do you even care what someone else's butt looks like? If we could go forwards in time, I swear our future selves would think that we all went mad for a time, obsessing over what someone else looks like beneath their clothes and labouring under the misapprehension that it was somehow doing us some good.

If your particular interest is *your* body and how to make it work best for you, follow people who will show you how to work out in a way that you enjoy and is fun. The second it starts to feel anything other than informative or fun, unfollow and delete. Walk away. You're *inviting* them into the palm of your hand, and they don't have to stay there.

Consider Your Online Behaviour

This also works the other way round. If you follow someone and find that *everything* they do pisses you off, don't sit there fuming and judging and firing off nasty comments and DMs telling them so. That doesn't do either of you any good at all.

You've chosen to follow them into their home, to have a look around. If you don't like what you see in there – if you hate the way it's decorated, and the things they talk about in their kitchen get on your nerves – you have the power to leave. To walk away. Do it. Don't stand in their home shouting at them. You wouldn't do it in real life, so don't do it online.

You see, it's not just who we follow online that can put us in a bad headspace, it's also how *we behave* online that does so. There are people who say things online that they wouldn't dream of saying in real life. And if that's you, it doesn't mean that you're being brave or courageous. It's the opposite – you're being mean and hiding behind your phone and your keyboard.

After that momentary feeling of *That'll show her, the uppity little bitch!*, you may walk around feeling pretty good about yourself, but it's not helping you. It's not a good way to be. So don't do it. It will start eating away at you and make you feel even worse about yourself, which in turn will become a cycle of lowering your self-esteem so you don't believe in yourself any more, which will make you even angrier with the world! That in turn will make you feel weak, which will make you feel scared.

All of this will take you further away from your ultimate goal of believing that you can do whatever it is you're scared of trying. You may feel angry and jealous of people who are brave and believe in themselves – but *you* can do that too!

2. What Do You Watch?

Now by this I mean the TV, the news websites and the newspapers you read. Sometimes we like to kid ourselves into believing that to be smart and on top of things, we need to know what's going on every second of the day in every corner of the world. We don't, and here's why – not all news is news. In fact, I'd say that 90 per cent of news is *not* news. Whaat?

Back in the olden days, when there was one TV channel and a couple of newspapers to choose from, the time devoted to getting the correct information across was precious. The production and printing of newspapers was an expensive enterprise, so the information had to be correct at the time of 'going to press'. Facts needed to be checked and sources verified, and a balanced viewpoint had to be given because editors took their responsibility of being the bearer of news seriously. Of course, the newspaper you bought would always have a certain bias – it's always been so – but in the main, the stories were fairly and correctly reported.

And then rolling news arrived and 24 hours of content had to be found. Suddenly it wasn't enough simply to report on events after they happened; instead, reporting was expected *as* it happened, which didn't leave much time to evaluate and separate fact and balance from conjecture.

Opinion about what was happening was then sought, and experts were brought in to discuss their thoughts on the news. And then, those opinions became facts that overtook the news itself. Because let's be honest, it's much more interesting to listen to people have an argument about something than it is to think about the actual thing itself, right?

While listening to an informed debate is interesting and gives us a chance to learn a different perspective on something we'd never normally pay much attention to, it's now very rare for this to be the case. The beast must now feed itself, so the newspapers and news channels fall over themselves not only to be the first to report on the news, but also to fill their pages and airtime with opinion and conjecture about it. And the bigger and scarier the predictions the better, because it means more people will tune in, click on or buy!

Be Selective

Where does this leave you? Stressed, anxious, overwhelmed and not knowing who to believe. So, have a think about the news sites you look at and the papers you read; are they balanced, or do they add fuel to the fire by making you feel anxious and overwhelmed? Limit the number of news sources you engage with and the time you engage with them. Remember: 24-hour news is *not all news*; much of it is opinion and conjecture.

There are incredible documentaries and programmes available to us that give a measured perspective on the way things are in the world. You'll find them on the usual TV channels and also on streaming sites such as Netflix, Apple and Amazon Prime.

**Take the time to watch and listen to things
that enlighten, not just frighten.**

It's important to remind yourself that there's always hope – this will feed the self-belief and courage that it's possible for you to be a part of the change you want to see in the world, rather than a terrified bystander.

Be selective about what you watch away from the news, too. We're all different – my husband and I have very different ideas about what makes for relaxing TV! At the end of a long day, I like to watch something light but big-hearted, which is why I choose feelgood dramas to uphold my belief that there are good people in the world – something that the news seems determined to prove otherwise.

He likes to watch shouty dramas in which everyone's either a zombie or very angry and determined to kill each other – the complete opposite of what I need to see! He feels: *At least our life isn't as bad as that*, while I feel: *Ahh, what a lovely, kind thing so-and-so did in tonight's episode*. Either way, we both climb into bed with the same sense of self-belief and the courage of our convictions – we just have a different way of getting there!

3. Who Do You Spend Your Time with?

Now that we've talked about spending time online and in front of the screen, let's have a think about the people in real life with whom you're spending your time and how they make you feel.

Why are you with them? Is it a relationship or a friendship you've drifted into or one you chose to be in? This may seem like a strange way of looking at things – after all, people don't tend to come into your life by choice. You meet someone and feel that you like them, and they like you, so you start doing things together. Before you know it, they've become your friend.

Most of us have friends that we're with through habit or convenience. Perhaps they're people at your workplace who make your job bearable, maybe even fun, because you laugh at the same things. Or they're a friend you've been paired up with simply because they're in a relationship with someone your partner likes – we've all been in that situation, where it's just easier to drift into something that you'd not normally do because it makes life more pleasant for everyone if you all get along.

This can become difficult when you find that you're expected to want to spend time with this person, even though you've nothing in common and in truth, you find them really quite irritating. I know people who've spent *years* having friends like these, sitting with a smile on their face through torturous dinner parties and nights out while their partners had a whale of a time, turning a blind eye to how earth-shatteringly boring or annoying this 'friend' is.

If you're in this situation, try and find a way to be honest about how you're feeling – even if it's just with your partner. I know how difficult this can be, as it's so deeply ingrained in us to simply sit it out – but how are we supposed to do that when we're also told that life is too short to do things we don't want to do?

The Courage to Say No

A friend of mine went through a scenario like this recently, but she *did* have the courage and self-belief she needed to step aside. She and her husband were invited to a big event and the couple hosting it had also invited people that my friend knew were extremely challenging to be around, especially once the drinks started flowing. This wasn't a guess – she'd experienced it before and she just didn't want to go to the event, even though she'd be the only one in their group to decline.

She weighed up the pros and cons. It was only a few hours out of her life and although it would be torturous and she'd rather have root canal work than go, she knew she could grin and get through it. Or, she could have the courage to politely decline the invitation and spend the evening doing something she'd rather do instead. She took a deep breath and said she couldn't make it as she had other commitments.

Her husband backed her up, understanding how uncomfortable the evening would have made her, and went along on his own. Questions were asked, eyebrows were raised and gossip was spoken, but my friend shrugged it all off. She's spent many years working hard to build up her own sense of who she is and to have the courage to stand by it.

Having the courage to say no doesn't mean you have to be rude – I personally don't have an issue with a polite reply cased in a little white lie. Sometimes, life really is too short.

Journal Time ✍

In your journal, write a list of the people in your friendship group and then remind yourself how you got together and why you're still together. Is it just easier to stay friends? Was it expected that you'd stay friends forever, just because you once got on well? Maybe you've changed, maybe they've changed; maybe the two of you just don't have anything in common any more and you're tired of pretending you do. It's a horrible feeling when you come to this realization, but while you're going through this process of building up your confidence, try to limit the time you spend with that friend.

If you don't have people in your life right now who lift you up, follow people online who give you what you need, until you have the confidence to make your friendship circle as uplifting. Cast your net a little wider and join some new groups: dip your toe in and see how it feels to meet new people.

Look for those friends who champion you and choose them. Stop trying to win over the ones who don't look out for you.

And don't take it too seriously – this is simply about spending some time with people and examining how you feel about that time. You should hopefully feel good, have some fun and either laugh, learn or both while you're together. Think of the 80/20 rule: spend 80 per cent of your time, both physically and digitally, with people who lift you and 20 per cent with the rest – if you must see them.

4. How Do You Spend Quality Time in Your Relationship?

You'd hope that the person you've chosen to be your romantic partner in life is someone whose thoughts and emotions are similar to your own, so that you understand, empathize with and support each other. This is the person who you're probably going to be spending more time with than anyone else, so it stands to reason that you'll be affected by them and their attitude and outlook.

Have you given this much thought? Or have you drifted into a relationship of convenience, where it's just easier to be with each other than not? Even if there are no real problems within your relationship – as in there's no abuse, anger or neglect – simply living in disconnect is unsettling.

As humans we have a basic need to feel connected and understood, as well as seen and heard, and if we aren't getting these needs met by the person we've chosen to love above all others, this will affect our sense of self-belief. This could be something that your partner is unaware of; or, with a bit of prompting, you may find that they too are feeling a little lost and fearful.

Communication is the only way to resolve this – so find the time and space to talk to each other. We've recently emerged from a very tough global experience, and it's natural that this will have had an impact on our relationships.

The power of unlocking your courage and rediscovering your inner self-confidence is even more beautiful when it's done in unison with someone you love. Talk to them. Give them the opportunity to grow with you; it could be the most powerful joint experience you've ever had.

5. How Do You Spend Quality Time with Yourself?

And finally, remember that *you* are a key component in your five to thrive. Spending time thinking about the people and voices that you surround yourself with is important, but so too is remembering that your lack of courage and self-belief also stem from the *internal* voice you listen to.

Shame and vulnerability are two of our most powerful emotions, and right now, they're being triggered on an hourly basis, if not more, which is enough to send even the most confident of us into a tailspin of fear and self-doubt. The shame of not being our best self, looking our best, living our best life (whatever the hell that's supposed to mean) in the ridiculous age of Instagram reality has seeped into our daily lives as well as our online ones.

No matter how many people you follow or are friends with who say great, encouraging things to you, there will be a small part of what they do that makes you feel bad about yourself because you don't feel you're doing things as well as they are. Let that go; you aren't them and they aren't you.

We're all now so afraid of getting things wrong that we're in danger of becoming paralyzed into inaction. There is such shame in failing. Oh, my goodness – making a mistake can now get you cancelled, vilified, cowering in the online version of the stocks with strangers throwing metaphorical rotten food at you.

The world has literally gone crazy, with people blaming and shaming anyone who's either made a mistake or has behaved in a way that the loud online 'shouterati' have deemed offensive or inappropriate, rarely bothering to check the truth or validity in whatever it is that they're so angry with or about.

In this bizarre 'emperor's new clothes' mentality, no one wants to be the first to raise their hand and say: 'This doesn't make any sense. It's causing way more harm than the good it had the potential to do.'

People are now so afraid of being seen in the 'wrong' light, of doing the 'wrong' thing, that they're making themselves ill. The very thing that was supposed to set us free – the 'social' side of this virtual media – now has us locked in fear.

This is having a huge impact on our relationship with ourselves, as well as on our relationship with the world outside of 'us'. It's keeping us locked in a world of fear where our metaphorical tiger no longer prowls at our cage door to keep us safe. She's inside with us, cowering in the corner and waiting for the madness outside to end.

My biggest tip for having a better relationship with yourself? Step away from the virtual world. Live your life in your present.

Think about it this way. When do you feel at your most beautiful? At your happiest? At your most in touch with yourself? It's when you're totally absorbed in what you're doing, or who you're doing it with. It can be when you're on your own – listening to music that makes you happy, walking in the sunshine – or looking into the eyes of someone you love during your most intimate moments together.

If, at that moment, you're worried about what one judgemental friend or thousands of strangers would make of you, you're *missing the point* of being alive.

Your relationship with yourself is the most powerful relationship you'll ever have in the one life you're blessed to be given. Love yourself as those who truly love you do – for all that you are and all that you're capable of. Because you're worth it. *You just need to believe it.*

***

Well done for completing today, and for hacking into these parts of your life that were holding you down. I hope you now feel free! That freedom is going to feel even more powerful tomorrow when we look at love. And not just any old love, oh no. You're going to learn how to love the most important person in your life: yourself.

DAY 6

'I Love You'

'Love yourself first and everything else just falls into line. You really have to love yourself to get anything done in this world.'

Lucille Ball

How many of us spend most of our lives, or in some cases, *all* our lives, waiting for someone else to make us feel loved, protected and brave? It starts with the love of our parents who, if we're fortunate, make us feel this way.

From the room in my home where I write, as I sit at my desk near the window to the world outside, I see parents taking their young children to school every day. There are many young families on the street where I live, and every morning follows the same routine: children giggling, skipping and scootering along and parents carrying bags and chatting as they literally and figuratively carry the weight while their children dance ahead carefree.

The body language alone is interesting to watch; I see it change as the children grow, and in the outline of the adults who walk past on their way to work, to the shops, to collect their children from school at the end of the day.

The older we become, the less we skip and laugh, which is understandable – we'd get some very strange looks if we did! Our worries and concerns become deeper and heavier as we grow up, and the distance between us and our parents naturally stretches as we push ourselves out into the world, finding our own way.

But in that push away, in that natural move towards independence, we lose the security blanket of love that our parents wrapped us in. So, we look for it elsewhere: from our friends, who become our second family; we confide in, laugh with, argue with and get excited about our future with them.

And from our online 'friends', who have us consumed with hope that they'll 'like' us by pressing a little heart or a thumbs-up sign on their screen, showing us that they approve of something we've done, or how we look, or what we're wearing. Every time someone we don't know, and will never meet, signals to us that they 'like' us, a rush of endorphins floods our system, in the way it does when we receive love.

Harnessing the Power of Self-Love

Our need for love is what makes us so beautifully human. It's what drives us to connect, to bond, to create. It's a kind of madness in a way. Think of how it makes us behave when we first fall into it; the little amount of sleep we can survive on; the rush of emotions that whirl through us. We can't eat, and we can't think straight. All we can think about is the person we've fallen in love with! That raw vulnerability and openness of heart, mind and spirit is intoxicating.

So, it makes total sense that we spend our time in constant search of the 'other' that will make us feel this way. That other is in the first instance human, but if we can't find it in another person, we go looking elsewhere – online for the likes and clicks from humans we'll never meet, know or touch, but also in the form of shopping, food, drink, gambling, working. We're constantly craving something outside of us that no one has ever shown us has been inside us all along: love. Or to be more specific, self-love.

Self-love is a term that makes a lot of us recoil. What the hell does it even mean? Does it mean masturbation? Yes, when thinking about it sexually, but of course that's not all it means. Taking control of your own pleasure and not relying on someone else to make you feel good, sexually or in any other way, is a hugely powerful tool. It's vital if you're ever going to have a strong relationship with anyone else too, because how can you let them know what you like if you don't even know yourself?

It can be a bit cringey to think about masturbation as a powerful thing, as it's been tied up with guilt and shame for so long. But why is it shameful to make yourself feel good? Consider it this way: this shame that we're raised to feel at the idea of making ourselves feel good has literally taken the control of our own pleasure, our own happiness, out of our hands.

Society has raised us to think that the only happiness that counts is that which comes from another person or thing. Any joy we create ourselves is selfish, which leads to feelings of guilt, shame and yes, *fear*. A deep, primal fear of being cast aside by our tribe for looking after our own joy. And this can be in any form – I don't mean it sexually in this instance; I mean it in any decision we make that society doesn't universally approve of.

Loving Ourselves Every Day

Let's put the whole idea of sexual self-love to one side now and focus on us as people, as humans on a planet spinning in space, busy comparing ourselves to every other human on the planet and wishing that they would show us the love and compassion for which we're so desperate. Self-love in this sense is the most powerful tool that any of us can hold, because again, it takes us from a place of needing love from an outside source to simply accepting and enjoying it for the beautiful experience it is.

The obvious definition of self-love is doing something for ourselves – maybe a little spa day, get our nails done. But I think this is quite an old-fashioned way of looking at things. It smacks of 'why not go and treat yourself to something nice, sweetheart?' and then get back to real life and feeling shit about yourself. And can I just say, this is from someone who *loves* a spa day – I'm first in line for a massage and a fluffy robe! So, this isn't a diss on relaxing experiences, not at all; it's about how we view treating ourselves as a person who deserves to feel good about themselves.

Self-love should be something that's done daily, not every now and then for birthdays, with a little pat on the head. If you're thinking, *I haven't the faintest clue where to start with this*, here are a few suggestions.

Practise Acceptance

A feeling of acceptance is something that pretty much all of us struggle with; I think it's fair to say that most of our stress comes from wishing things were different and raging against our powerlessness to change them.

The first step towards changing our mindset when it comes to how things are versus how we think they should be is finding gratitude. Every day, even when it's shitty. In fact, especially when it's shitty because that's when you need the biggest amount of love thrown your way, and sometimes there's no one to give it to you other than yourself.

We don't have to look too far to find affirmations and positive quotes telling us that we deserve good things to happen to us. They're all true, and we need to hear them when we're feeling ground down by life and the difficulties it throws at us. However, those very affirmations also need to be absorbed with balance.

I don't believe that there's a finite amount of goodness in the world and that someone else's good fortune means that there's less of it to go round for everyone else. There's enough for all. But I've also come to accept that the same goes for misfortune. Just as there's enough love, there's also enough pain, and I'm as deserving of it as anyone else. Fortune and misfortune come to us all.

I brought this up at a recent session I had with my coach, while we were talking about some challenges I'm experiencing. She laughed and said, 'That's because you're a Growth Incarnation.' We'd never spoken like this before, and I wasn't sure what she meant.

She explained that she feels there are people in this world who are born to be challenged and that their purpose is to find solutions to these challenges – to grow through them and pass on the lessons. And then there are people who are born *never* to be challenged, whose lives will appear to everyone else to be plain sailing; but they will never learn, and they will never grow. Their pleasure and pain will be different, but they will still experience it.

Her simple acceptance of this made me think, and it reminded me of a meditation I do in the mornings. I do guided meditations, depending on how I feel or what I sense I need that day; sometimes I need to receive guidance or support, so I choose accordingly.

Some of my favourite meditations are created by an Australian man called Jason McGrice, who I found on the Insight Timer app. When I was going through my particularly difficult time a few years ago and was struggling with unresolved pain from my past and an extremely challenging present, I'd hear him say: 'Everything is perfect in this present moment' and a part of me would *rage* against it because that couldn't have been further from how I felt!

How could things be perfect when I was in so much pain? And then one day, after listening to Jason's meditation daily for months, something in me shifted and I realized that he was right. I realized that at that moment, everything was exactly as it should be. I was hurting, and there were things happening in my life that didn't feel fair, but that didn't mean I was any more or less deserving of pain than anything else. This was simply my share of it, just as I've had my share of good things that have happened to me.

When we think of things that happen to us that cause us pain, we feel we don't deserve them. But do we ever flip this on its head and think of the good things that happen to us that we also don't deserve? There are just as many times when good things happen to us that we don't deserve.

The Illusion of Fairness and Unfairness

Right now, you may be in the middle of something that's hurting your heart and seems so unfair, which *is* so unfair! And it can feel impossible to think of something good which happened to you that was also undeserved. But trust me, it's the only way to balance it out.

What do I mean by something good that you didn't deserve? It can be anything, and it's as individual as you are, but it could be that you were born to kind parents who loved you; or that you were born in a part of the world where you had access to clean water and the right to an education. Or it could be a chance meeting that led to finding true love – you didn't deserve to stumble on such riches any more than your best friend who never seems to.

What's so interesting about how we behave as humans, and what I think separates us from the rest of the animal kingdom, is the emotional attachment we give to life events, placing them in categories of 'fair' and 'not fair'. Why is it more unfair for something bad to happen to you than to someone else? And why do you deserve to have good things happen to you more than anyone else?

This is something I know I've personally been guilty of; for most of my life I've had a giant moral compass that's swung wildly at any notion of something not being fair. My parents tell me that at the age of seven I was furious with my primary school head teacher for awarding first, second and third prizes when we only had four people in each class (I went to a tiny school).

I told her she was being unfair because there would be one child who would never win anything because they weren't good at running or whatever, and because the class was so small, they were the only one left out, every single time. I didn't have an issue with there being a first, second and third place – I understood that not everyone could win – but with the fact that there being only four of us meant one poor person would end up feeling disproportionately bad.

Even at that age, I felt that if there had been 30 of us not winning and the deserving top three getting a prize it would have been in proportion. I didn't know what proportion was, of course: I just knew that this felt unfair and cruel. Apparently, my unimpressed head teacher looked down at me and told me that the pupils needed to learn not to be a 'bad loser'.

I carried this feeling around pretty much my whole life, railing against life's unfairnesses: not just when they were directed at me but at anyone. My heart still bursts with pain when I see anything that isn't just, or right.

But then I realized, not too long ago, that both the teacher and I were missing the point. What does fair have to do with anything? It's not just about being a 'bad loser' when life shits all over you, or about railing at injustice when we experience it – these things are important and it's vital that we speak up.

We must accept that there will be times in our lives when things happen to us, both good and bad, that we don't deserve.

It's about acting with self-love in both of those scenarios and what we do about them. They say that integrity is doing the right thing even when no one's watching. But it's also doing the right thing when things happen to you that you don't deserve. Pay it forwards when it's good and when it's bad, accept that you're just as deserving of bad fortune as anyone else.

Absolutely, you need to fight against it and do your best to overcome it and stop it happening again – to yourself and to others. But that's not the same as feeling hurt because it isn't 'fair'. It's life and it's something we'll all experience. However, we tend to feel that because we're good people we deserve good things and don't deserve bad.

What I'm getting at is this: we don't deserve anything, and we deserve everything. It is what it is.

Heal Pain with Self-Love and Compassion

You may be wondering what this has to do with loving yourself. Bear with me, because I hope you'll soon see that it has everything to do with it. If you're in a place right now where you're hurting, it may not make much sense, but there's a comfort in accepting that it would be no fairer to expect someone else to go through what you are, than it is for you to go through it.

The way to get through it, however, is to *give yourself love*. I really struggled with this as well at first. It seemed like an oxymoron – I was in so much emotional pain that even my body hurt with it. I was going through a terrible time with one of our children (which will remain private) and it was causing me sleepless nights through worry, stress and turmoil.

My left eye kept twitching, my jaw hurt from clenching my teeth during what little sleep I was getting, and my limbs felt so heavy and my skin so sore that even going for a walk was an effort. At that moment, when I didn't think I could mentally or physically take any more stress, Nick and I came to the sinking conclusion that our business wasn't earning money as quickly as we needed it to, to keep us afloat.

Technical issues had put us months behind with the launch of our app, and our burgeoning waiting list was wilting as we didn't want to take on new clients only to move them around a short while later; we wanted them to join our shiny, sleek membership where they'd get amazing value, not the clunky one that our loyal founder members were hanging in there with because they loved and supported us.

We kept being reassured that it would happen 'by the end of the week', but then another week would go by, and another, and another, each one costing us money we were quickly running out of.

A joint venture we'd been working on fell through at the eleventh hour, costing us thousands in wasted time and money, and another venture didn't make the return it had promised. The PR jobs that I'd been offered and was counting on to give us a financial buffer while the business gained momentum had gone. Every single one of them dropped me the day I left my job because I wasn't on TV any more.

Rock Bottom

In short, *none* of our ships had come in. We felt that every time we were so *nearly there*, the goal posts were moved further away. 'Nearly there' was great, but it wouldn't pay the mortgage. I'd already taken out a loan against the house, sold our car and taken the tax holiday offered by HMRC because of the pandemic. But soon that would all end, and we wouldn't have the money to pay it.

The day we realized we had to put our home on the market was a dark one. Nick had been getting edgy and prickly, and this culminated in a *huge* one-sided argument about something neither of us can remember, at the end of which he stomped away sulkily, leaving me in tears.

After a sleepless night, Nick said sorry, and admitted he'd been holding in all the stress and frustration he was feeling that things weren't going as we'd hoped, and it had all come out in the wrong way. We hugged it out, but I felt exhausted and bruised and spent the morning quietly getting on with things to try and keep my mind off everything that was going on. It was over a coffee that I finally said it out loud: 'We're going to have to sell the house.' Nick nodded, grimly.

It sounds stupid, but I didn't care so much about the house; it was the thought of walking away from my garden that moved me to tears. I'd put blood, sweat and tears into creating an oasis of sweet, jasmine-fragranced, wisteria-covered peace and quiet that was my sanctuary from the world. It had taken me nine years to nurture and grow everything to the point where it was all just right.

My beautiful back porch, which had been my happy place for almost a decade – how could I leave somewhere that was such a part of me? The roses I'd personally spent hours spraying, pruning and teasing into life now grew in a beautiful arch over my front door. They were like children to me, which I know sounds crazy, but ask any gardener and they'll know what I mean.

I didn't feel shame about having to sell my home; I understood that these things happen every day. My main emotions were disappointment and sadness. It was a kind of grief because I'd always told myself that the day I left that house would be the day

I either moved to live by the sea because the kids had all left home or moved into a mansion because life had become so great! Instead, I was selling it because I needed the money.

Love Is the Key

Why am I telling you this in a chapter about self-love? Because, and I know we all have different things going on in our lives that are hurting us and mine may seem like annoying small fry compared to yours, the hardest part of dealing with all of this was the pain that came from the problem with one of the children.

I felt so shut out, afraid for them and unable to help them, and losing our home seemed to compound it all. My garden represented all the nurturing I'd given my family; it had been my safe space when I got divorced. I'd raised my children in the house, and now it felt like everything was falling apart.

I wanted to lie in bed and not move – just sleep and get someone to wake me up when the bad stuff was over. I'd been through enough already; I'd had more than my fair share. And then I realized that I needed to apply the rule of fairness to myself once again. I needed to give myself the love that I so desperately needed from the world.

It felt wrong to try to be cheerful and upbeat when so much was going wrong, but it was vital. Not in a falsetto, wild-eyed, 'It'll all be alright!' kind of way; I just needed to believe that everything would work out for the best.

After all, what was a 'fair share' of pain? I've had much less than some and more than others. If that's the case, then surely that sounds about right. And allowing myself to be swallowed up by grief over my child and stress over my home and business meant that I couldn't see anything other than pain. Which I knew from experience wasn't doing me any good at all.

I needed to feel love, gratitude and self-compassion. I needed to fill myself up with so much of this that it flowed out of me and spilled onto everyone around me, especially those I loved. I needed it to fill every part of me, so that I could look up at the huge tiger of fear who was pressing me down and drown out her roar with my love.

Love was the key to unlocking my courage and reclaiming my power, and so I started to create it for myself.

Meditate into Self-Love

Meditation is something that was part of my routine anyway, but now I made it my daily practice to work on noticing, feeling and acknowledging everything I was grateful for. I needed to fill myself up with love – for myself, for everything I had and for the people in my life. It was *hard*, and if you're in this space right now, it will be hard for you too.

If meditation isn't something that you normally do, then it will feel very strange at first. I'm going to describe it to you here in a way I've used many times before as I think it normalizes something that can seem a bit alien but is in fact incredibly powerful.

To me, meditation is a way of connecting with myself at a deep level that no one else can, only me, and I see it as one of the most powerful tools in my kit box when it comes to self-love. Here's how it works:

1. Get Ready

Find somewhere quiet to sit where you won't be disturbed for at least 15 minutes. This may not be simple, so find wherever works for you. I think meditation works best in the morning as it sets you up well for the rest of the day but do it when and where works best for you. There are days when the only space I can get 15 minutes' peace from the world is on my bathroom floor with the door locked. I bring in a cushion, so I don't get pins and needles in my bum and legs, and off I go.

You can sit in a chair or on the floor, wherever you're comfortable. I like to lean against something, otherwise my back hurts, and as you don't get extra points for being tough, I'd recommend you do the same. Don't tuck yourself up in bed, though, as falling asleep, while lovely and very important, is not the same as meditating.

Set a timer for 10 minutes. I'd recommend the one on your phone as it's silent. A kitchen timer ticking away next to you won't work at all. If you can set the sound to something gentle, like a soft bell, then do that. You don't want to be jolted out of your reverie by a shrieking buzzer.

Get yourself settled and comfy because you'll be sitting still for a while. Rest your hands on your lap; you can have them facing upwards in the 'receiving' position, but you don't need to do hold them in any special way, just however is comfortable.

2. Breathe into Awareness

We'll begin by taking a few deep breaths. You'll be amazed at how much better you feel by doing that; just getting some air deep into the lungs clears your head and reminds you that despite the fact we do it from the moment we're born until the moment we die, most of us are not very good at breathing!

Close your eyes and breathe deeply and gently, in through your nose and out through your mouth. You can do this a few times; three times as a minimum, but 10 times is great. You may feel strange doing this, but it's very powerful.

As you breathe in, and with your eyes closed, say in your mind, *I love you.* See yourself in your mind's eye, sitting wherever you're sitting, giving yourself the gift of this time and space to renew your energy and nourish yourself.

See it for what it is: you're giving this gift to yourself, and you're wholly deserving of it. I sometimes feel pins and needles release in my head as I realize I've been holding everything in, my teeth unknowingly clenched, and the feeling of being loved is like being held in my own arms. It's made me cry before as I've let go, and because I'm on my own I can let it happen – I'm not being strong for anyone else.

3. Kapalabhati Breathing

If you really want to get things going, try this:

Still seated, raise your arms in the air and breathe in deeply through your nose; then, as you quickly lower your arms, breath out sharply through your nose. Do this about 30 times, quickly, raising your arms up and down, up and down, so your heart starts pumping, while breathing in and out through your nose. (It's a good idea to give your nose a good blow into a tissue first, for obvious reasons.)

You can take this to another level; it's a little more advanced, so take it really easy at first. This is a beginner's guide if you like. It's called Kapalabhati breathing, and it involves using your stomach muscles to push the air out of your body.

Leave your hands on your lap and take a deep, passive, slow breath in. Focus on your lower abdominal muscles and practise pulling them in sharply as you exhale through your nose. Try and do three sharp exhales after one in breath.

Take it easy at first – it's tricky and will feel strange. Once you get the hang of it, try a deep in breath and then five sharp exhales through your nose. Then try getting up to 10 sharp exhales through your nose, followed by a deep inhale through your nose.

You only need to do this cycle three or four times to feel a little lightheaded, but it also really clears your mind by giving a massive surge of oxygen to your whole body. Like I say, take it easy with this one. If you'd like to try Kapalabhati breathing in a bit more depth, YouTube is awash with tutorials on it. I first heard about it on a yoga retreat many years ago and once I got the hang of it and stopped worrying about snot shooting out my nose, I loved it! (Top tip, always have a tissue handy.)

4. Body Scan

Now close your eyes and let your breathing return to normal. Pay attention to the sounds that you hear around you; familiarize yourself with them so they don't disturb you. It sounds crazy, but simply acknowledging the sounds – 'That's a dripping tap. That's my neighbour's dog barking. That's a delivery van reversing' – will stop them becoming petty annoyances that prod you in the face while you're trying to relax. You've acknowledged them and they've nothing to do with what you're doing right now, so let them go.

In your mind, start to scan down your body, beginning at the top of your head. Talk to yourself as you do so – it may sound like you're listing each part of your body, from your feet to your head. Focus on what your body feels like, but in passing; don't linger on any niggles.

Ask yourself, *Why am I doing this?* Not in a grumpy tone of voice, but in a matter-of-fact 'reminding yourself' one. I tend to say to myself, *I'm doing this today to make me relax, and to help me cope with things better.* Other times, I say that I'm doing it because I'm feeling stressed, or low, or anxious. Or I say I want to be a more patient mother and partner. Sometimes I say I'm doing it because it feels good. There are no rules.

Ask yourself, *How do I feel?* Now this is interesting. Usually, we're so programmed to say 'fine' when asked this question that we don't really ask ourselves how we're feeling in any one moment. We're either trying to hide it (annoyed) or enjoy it (happy) and we don't really own up to it or put a name to it.

But no one's going to hear you – this is just for you – and I can't tell you how liberating it is to say to yourself, *I'm pissed off today. I'm in a really bad mood.* Be honest and say to yourself: *I'm feeling grumpy today. I'm stressed today.* No one is going to judge you.

In fact, it's interesting to pause for a moment and think about how you're feeling. And it can be as liberating to say *I'm annoyed* as it is to say *I'm feeling calm today. I'm feeling happy.* You're not trying to change it, or do anything about it, or trying to impress anyone. It's just how you're feeling right now, and that's fine.

5. Deal with Random Thoughts

By now, you should be feeling a little more relaxed. Focus again on your breath. Feel the air coming in through your nose, going down into your chest, and notice how your chest feels as it expands and contracts as the air comes in and out of your body. Do this a few times and then start to count each breath. Count 'one' as it goes in, 'two' as it goes out, and so on. Do this until you get to 10 and then start over again.

Now that *sounds* very simple, but it's where the mindfulness part of meditation comes in. This is the point where your brain decides it would rather drip-feed an annoying tune by an artist whose name you can't quite remember into your head. Then you'll remember that you forgot to buy that birthday card you were supposed to. Or to get bread. And, Oh God, did you pay the gas bill? What number were you on again?

You get the gist. This is where the breathing and the counting come in: to give your mind a rest from all this stuff. It's important stuff, obviously (especially the annoying song), but you just don't need to think about it right now.

When this happens – and it will, every time: this bit doesn't stop, you just get better at stepping away from the chatter – I like to think of these thoughts as children. A random thought is like a child who rushes in and demands instant attention for something they think is *hugely* important but can actually wait a moment because it's fairly simple – like a stick they found or a TikTok video of a cat. You're able to say kindly: *That's nice. I'll look at it in a moment, sweetheart*, and off they go (hopefully).

What you don't say is: *No, go away! I won't listen to you. Stop it. I won't look... aargh, I'm looking! I've forgotten where I was!* But that's exactly what you do when you try and force your brain to ignore the annoying thoughts as they pop up, tugging on your mind's sleeve and demanding instant attention.

When you meditate, you train yourself to say to your thoughts: *I know you're there, but I'm doing this right now and I'll deal with you in a minute.* And the pesky thought, rather than hanging on to your arm and whining until you pay it some attention, wanders off to draw on walls or flush things down the toilet, or whatever it is that thoughts do while no one's listening to them.

6. Acknowledge Your Feelings

You'll also have random feelings rise up while you're breathing and counting. They're rarely happy ones but if they are, then excellent, they can stay. Sometimes a thought can pop into your head that will remind you of something that made you angry. So now you're feeling anger. Acknowledge it and accept it. It is what it is, and that's where you are right now.

I like to think of the feelings that crop up as moody teenagers. They feel that the whole world is against them, and nobody understands, so they mope around, being rude and messy until they get a rise out of someone and can have a good old row and get things off their chest.

That's what feelings are doing when they lurch into your brain. And in the same way as you'd deal with a moody teen, you acknowledge this feeling of anger but say you're busy right now and you'll deal with it later. And off they will go, grumbling that nobody's interested in them.

Keep breathing in and out, counting each breath, up to 10, then start again.

It sounds like an awful lot of work, doesn't it? All that sitting there breathing and counting and telling your thoughts and feelings to get lost! But here's the thing: you would have had all those thoughts and feelings anyway, but you'd have had them mooching around your head while you were trying to get on with your day and cope with the things that really needed to be dealt with, on top of all of that.

All this explains why at the end of every day, you feel knackered and ratty with everyone: your brain is worn out from dealing with real stuff on the outside and nonsense on the inside.

This is your chance to let your brain have a rest and switch off for a while. And when it does, amazing things happen to you physically: the stress hormones in your body reduce. Even if you only manage to count to 10 a handful of times, your mind will still feel the benefit of having a rest, just for that short space of time.

Meditate every day and it will get easier because you'll know how to shush the annoying thoughts and feelings. It won't work every time; some days they'll keep banging on and on and you can't help but stop counting and give in to them. That's fine. Try again later, or the next day, and don't beat yourself up about it.

7. Wind Down

When your timer goes off after 10 minutes, let your mind wander for a few moments. Don't think about counting, or your breath – let it do whatever it wants; it will probably be quite happy just to stay where it is, and will normally sit quietly in your head, awaiting further instruction. After a few breaths, bring your awareness back to the sounds around you. You'll be amazed at what you blocked out while you were busy focusing on your breath – the dripping tap and the neighbour's dog were there all along.

Then focus on your body and start to notice how heavy it is, the weight of your body on the chair or the floor, your hands in your lap, your head on your shoulders. Again, you'll be amazed how you hadn't noticed this before.

Slowly open your eyes and let yourself readjust to being back in the room. Notice how you feel. Whatever you feel, it's okay; there's no right or wrong – it's just how you're feeling at this moment. Once you're ready, slowly get up and carry on with your day.

And that's it. It's simple, but it can be tricky, and you do need to keep trying with it. But trust me, it works. It won't make it all go away, or make you 'better', but it really will help. Sometimes all you can do is stop, give yourself some love and just believe you'll feel better.

Mirror Work

What I'm going to talk you through now is something that's been used for many years as a way of deeply connecting with ourselves and our sense of self-worth. It's a practice called mirror work and while it's very straightforward to do, most people find it difficult emotionally. The first time I tried to do it, I felt ridiculous. It felt strange, and weirdly, it made me angry rather than feeling love.

I came across mirror work while researching Louise Hay. Louise's work on healing our body and mind through the power of thought was years ahead of its time in Western ideology, and her legacy continues to live on through the publishing house she founded, Hay House – it's how you're reading this book right now! For more about Louise and her work, check out www.louisehay.com.

So, what does mirror work involve? It's simply standing, or sitting, in front of a mirror and *really* looking at yourself. Most of us, women in particular, find it very difficult to do this. Men (overall, there are exceptions, of course) seem to find it much easier to look at themselves and see things that they like – they don't appear to be instantly drawn to the parts of their body that they feel are lacking in the way that women do.

Perhaps this is biology; or perhaps it's down to the constant barrage of imagery and adverts pushing products to remove so-called 'problem areas' that women are under from the moment they wake up to the moment they go to bed. Or the influencers and others telling them that to be happy, they need to buy this, or have that, or look like this.

Looking or living in any way outside these parameters means you're lacking in some way, and – you've guessed it – you won't be 'liked'. Or worse, you won't be loved. Which brings about that feeling of fear again – this time, the fear of not being 'enough'.

I can speak only from my personal experience as a woman, but I know that my eyes are *instantly* drawn to the parts of me that I find lacking, or in abundance! If I'm doing mirror work in my bathroom, for example after getting out of the shower, I instantly see my stomach.

I see the puckered skin from two pregnancies and the flesh that's never pinged back. I see the numerous scars across my abdomen – the results of two emergency caesareans, two laparoscopies, three hernia repairs, including a full internal abdominal repair, and a full hysterectomy. My stomach is a battlefield of cuts, scars and strange-looking skin.

I see the cellulite, once restricted to my bottom but now spread across my thighs, stomach and upper arms. I look at how bloated I am; I'm 14 pounds heavier than I used to be – 14 pounds heavier than I want to be. I look at the silver roots sprinkled around my hairline, just days after my last colour. I look at the lines around my eyes that no cream can smooth.

I look at the pigmentation scattered across my chest and face, which began in pregnancy, re-appears in the summer heat and now seems to stay year-round. I look at the skin of my neck, which seems to have lost the spring in its step. In fact, that's what I look like: someone who's lost the spring in her step. It's something I find most frustrating – at the very moment when I've found my life's springtime internally, my outer body has decided to go into a wintry decline!

A Practice for Everyone

My husband, on the other hand, looks at himself in the mirror, pulls a slight Zoolander face, slaps his flat six-pack and grins at himself. Sometimes I look at his grey hair and the wrinkles around his eyes and wonder how and when we decided as a society that his grey hairs and wrinkles are okay and mine are not.

I asked him about mirror work one day, and he told me that it's already something that he does regularly. He looks in the mirror every morning and tells himself that he's great, mentally high-fives his reflection and carries on with his day feeling awesome. It clearly works because he's the most confident person I know, always feeling on top of things and in control.

However, I've also seen him at his most vulnerable, when his constant quest for outward perfection results in plunging self-doubt because his abs aren't as defined as he'd like and he feels bloated and out of sorts, when I can't see any difference in him at all.

My husband is much fitter than I am, much stronger, and he's dedicated to working out daily. His self-worth is every bit as wrapped up in how he looks as that of many women I know. Despite his bravado, I know that he sometimes feels as vulnerable as I do, and that he needs to look himself in the eye and tell himself that he's great in order to believe it again. So, mirror work is very much for everyone – it's not simply a pick-me-up for women when we're feeling a bit bleurgh.

Mirror work is something that I wanted to share with you because when it comes to the way we view ourselves, it's both powerful and transformative. I mean this figuratively as well as metaphorically – how we view what we see in the mirror is reflected in how we then face the world. Now it's your turn:

Your Mirror Work Challenge

In your bedroom or your bathroom, stand or sit in front of a mirror (you may want to lock the door). You can be fully clothed for this, but some people have found it powerful to do it naked. You don't have to do it naked if you'd rather not, or you can build up to it; whichever way you want to do it is fine. It's more about looking deeply into your own eyes than at any other part of your body. Here's what to do:

♦ Look at yourself in the mirror. Look at your face, your hair, your eyes, your mouth. *Really* look. Take it all in.

♦ Once you've got past the automatic response of looking at all the parts of yourself that you don't like, let the mind calm down and look at yourself as if you were someone else – someone you care for very much. Imagine that the person in front of you in the mirror isn't 'you' but a dear friend who's having a tricky time of things and is feeling a bit down on themselves.

♦ What would you say to that friend?

♦ How kind would you be to that friend?

♦ How much love would you give to that friend?

♦ Why aren't you doing the same thing to yourself?

Be that friend to yourself. Look at yourself with kindness and love. Look at yourself through the eyes of love. See yourself as so many people who love you see you, not just how the critical voice in your head sees you.

Let's take this deeper now. The second part of this challenge will feel strange, and it will take some getting used to, but stick with it.

Your 'I Love You' Challenge

The premise of this one is simple – look at yourself in the mirror, love the person you see standing in front of you, and then *tell* them so. I recommend doing this in a room in your home where you can close or even lock the door; to begin with, this will help you feel less silly, and after a while, it will give you the complete privacy you need to release all the emotions that this simple act will bring up.

I want you to do this challenge today, once you've finished reading this chapter; take yourself away, shut the door and do it. If you can't, or it's too difficult for you, come back to it tomorrow, or the next day, or the next, until you manage to do it.

It's a vital part of this powerful 10-day process and will have the biggest impact on you. Once you've done it, do it again the following day and continue until it becomes a normal part of your life. Here's what to do:

◆ Get in front of your mirror – you can be sitting, standing, fully clothed or bare, however you like. The important thing is to look yourself in your eyes and really see yourself.

♦ Look at yourself in the mirror and tell yourself, *I love you*. Then keep saying it: *I love you*. Say it as if you're telling a child who doesn't believe you. Gently. Lovingly. Repeatedly. Even when you start to squirm and wish it would stop (and *you* will feel this way), say it again.

♦ Tell yourself what you like about what you see. Your beautiful eyes. Your wide smile. The way your front tooth is a little bit crooked. It can be anything. See yourself as a loved one sees you. Love what you see. Keep going.

The hardest part of this will be looking into your own eyes as you tell your reflection *I love you*. It will feel strange, horrible even. You may feel sick, stupid, raw, vulnerable. I cried the first time I did it properly. I felt so sad that I'd been so cruel to this woman standing in front of me. I'd been so nasty; I'd said such horrible things to her, and she didn't deserve any of it.

I'd been just as bad to myself as the toxic, abusive people in my life had been. Every word they'd said to me had stuck, become lodged in my brain and had somehow become my truth. I believed what they'd said about me, and I'd turned the magnifying glass on myself, hating what I saw, not believing that anything I could see or do or be would ever be good enough to be acceptable.

I didn't see myself as those who loved me saw me; I saw only flaws, weakness. You may also feel this. Most people do, but that's what makes it so powerful.

Journal Time ✍

In your journal/notebook, write down how this experience made you *feel* – there's no right or wrong with this; it's your own private and personal experience. It may have felt awful, embarrassing, cringeworthy and so far out of your comfort zone that you're glad it's over. It also may have felt incredibly moving, raw and exposing.

· ·

Get Rid of the Rocks

When was the last time you looked at yourself as a lovable being? As someone who's worthy of being loved? So often, we give out love into the world – to our families and our friends – but over the years we build a wall around our heart, to protect ourselves from being hurt or let down. Sadly, that stops us from receiving the love we deserve from ourselves. *This is what makes us so afraid.*

It's easier to back away from anything that could possibly cause us more pain, to block it out and not look at it, than it is to risk being hurt. But if you know that you're loved, and that you're lovable, anything seems possible.

Look at the way children think they can accomplish anything when a parent tells them they believe in them – when they tell them that they're strong, beautiful and brave! Recapture that feeling – that spirit of being filled with love and optimism for the future.

Of course, as a child it's easier to be light and carefree because children don't have the same worries or concerns as an adult. But those worries or concerns that we as adults are dealing with don't make us any less worthy of love than a child. If you saw a child who was suffering, who was in pain, would you blame the child? Tell them that they deserve it? I'd like to think that you wouldn't.

Yet we continue to do this to ourselves, and then wonder why we don't feel that we have courage. We don't believe that we have it within us to do great things, or to think of a life away from the one we're living right now. Or we try to carry on with life while dragging around the fear and self-loathing that's become so ingrained in us, we don't even register it any more.

That's like trying to carry a bag of rocks uphill and berating yourself for not being strong enough. Put down the bag. Take out the rocks. And remind yourself how strong you've been to have carried them for so long.

But you aren't going to do that any more. And the very act of getting rid of those rocks will make you feel lighter, more energized and braver than you ever have before. How? Because finally, you've learned the true beauty and power of self-love.

Remind yourself that you're worthy of love:

You're lovable.

You're loved.

You just need to believe it.

Congratulations for completing today's challenge. It was difficult, and it may have made you feel incredibly raw. I want you to know that *I love you* for being brave enough to do this; for doing something that caused you pain because you *know* it will help you unlock your courage and reclaim your power.

***

You've come so far over these past few days, and I'm very proud of you! You're doing so well, even if right now it doesn't feel like it. Tomorrow is going to be powerful, too, but in a very different way. Among other things, you're going to ask yourself a simple question: 'What would I attempt to do if I knew I couldn't fail?' Your answer may surprise you.

DAY 7

What Are You Afraid of?

*'What would you attempt to do if you
knew you could not fail?'*
ROBERT SCHULLER

I've stuck this question on a notice board that sits in front of my desk. I see it every day and it reminds me that my commitment to having courage and believing in myself never stops. As we explored earlier, there are so many factors in our life that are wrapped up in fear, including our work, our relationships, our status and our perceived success or failure.

Interestingly, while success is something that most of us strive for because we think that life will somehow be 'better when...', it's also something which, subconsciously, we're afraid of.

The annoying thing about fear is that it tricks us into thinking we're the only ones who are feeling it. Fear is like a sneaky, manipulative, and nasty lover who takes up all your waking thoughts and emotions, only for you to discover that they've mistreated you: they've been unfaithful to you with every other person on the planet. And that in itself should be enough to make you want to kick fear's ass.

Here are our top 10 fears:

1. Fear of embarrassing ourselves

2. Fear of getting it wrong

3. Fear of people laughing at us

4. Fear of people judging us

5. Fear of rejection

6. Fear of getting hurt

7. Fear of leaving people behind if we succeed

8. Fear of losing friends and loved ones

9. Fear of the unknown

10. Fear of success – what if it's a fluke and we get found out?

Six Key Reasons behind Your Fears

I'll bet that you have at least one, or possibly all, of these fears. What if I told you that *everyone* has at least one, or possibly all, of them? Even the people who do brave things. You see, being brave doesn't mean you stop being afraid. It simply means that you care less about what might go wrong and much, *much* more about what might go right.

Let's dig into the main reasons you're afraid:

1. You're Worried about What Others Think

It doesn't matter if you're a 14-year-old schoolgirl or a 40-year-old businessman, at its root, this fear is the same. These 'others' you fear could be strangers who aren't brave enough to attempt *half* of what you would, yet they'll sit in the anonymous dark and slag you off. Or so-called friends who are jealous of your bravery and want to pull you into their fear and lack of self-belief to make themselves feel better. Or work colleagues who are threatened by you and will make life uncomfortable for you because your bravery is making them look afraid.

I heard a great quote that's been attributed to the Hollywood actor Christian Bale: 'If you have a problem with me, call me. If you don't have my number, then that means you don't know me well enough to have a problem.' *That right there* is how we should all be thinking about people who want to pull us down. Unless you really know and care about the person who's thinking badly of you, and they really know and care about you, they don't count. Think of it this way: *if you can't count on them, they don't count.*

Journal Time ✍

Write down *who* you're afraid of and *why*. Really unpick this. Where has this fear come from? Do these people love you and are they afraid for you because they want to protect you? In which case, it's up to you to reassure them that you know what you're doing and you're okay with it. If they don't love you, or even like you, why do you care what they think?

2. You Want to Avoid Feeling Scared

Who likes being scared? I don't mean in a 'watching horror movies' or 'going on roller coasters' kind of scared; I mean 'pushing yourself out of your comfort zone' kind of scared. *You just need to believe it* means understanding that feeling scared is natural when you're trying something that you may fail at, or which others may laugh at – it means learning how to feel scared but doing it anyway.

Just remember that *you're* in control. If you tried something and it didn't work out, see it as just that – something that didn't work out. If you've got something wrong, swallow your pride, say sorry and do something about it.

You need to face fear to overcome it, and if you keep avoiding it, it will always be there.

But if you stare it in the eye, it will pipe down and let you pass. Fear is the scary dog that's blocking your path. If you run from it, it'll chase you. If you face it, it'll lie down. It's scary, but you can do it. *So do it.*

Journal Time ✍

Think about what it is that you're afraid of right now and then ask yourself, *What can I do about this fear? How can I stare it down?* Don't just write down one answer. Really dig into this; write the first thing that comes into your head and then ask *And then what?* and write the answer to that. Do this over and over again, asking *and then what?* until you're genuinely out of ideas. You may think that you only have *one* answer, but you don't. Once you start asking yourself this, you'll discover that you have many, many answers.

3. You Think You Don't Deserve to Succeed

This fear can come from many different sources, but most of the time it's an external one that's been internalized. Hypercritical parents or teachers, unsupportive family members or loved ones, jealous peers – poison from an outside source has seeped into your psyche and taken root.

Journal Time ✍

Write about a time in your life when someone said things to you that made you feel unworthy, incompetent or undeserving. Who were they? Why do you think they said these things to you? What was the benefit to them?

Writing it down is a big step towards separating the emotional pull of how awful that person's words made you feel from seeing the reasoning behind their actions. Making you feel small was a way of making them feel more in control, more powerful. It's about them, it's not about *you*.

4. You Don't Want to Fail

The key thing to remember here is that most of the time, we aren't actually afraid of failing, we're afraid of *embarrassing ourselves*. The two are not the same thing, and the sooner you stop worrying about being embarrassed, the sooner you'll learn to embrace failure for the learning lesson that it is.

Journal Time ✍

Think about something that would make you feel embarrassed. Write it down and then really dig into it and how truly embarrassing it could be. Roll around in it; get hot and uncomfortable. Tap into the worst-case scenario level of embarrassment and then pile more on top.

Wonderful! You now have an embarrassment blueprint you can use if the shit ever hits the fan! And if this cringeworthy thing happens, you won't be fazed in the slightest because you've already had your dress rehearsal. The real thing, if it ever occurs, will be a piece of cake.

5. You Don't Want to Disappoint Anyone

Who is it that you're afraid of disappointing? Dig deep here and be honest. Is it your partner, your friends, your colleagues, yourself or your parents? Why is this? Was there a time when you did something that wasn't met with approval and it both stung and stuck with you? Is that what you're revisiting every time you think about trying to do something brave?

Journal Time ✍

Write a list of the people you love and who love you. This list can be as long or as short as you like – just make sure you include people you care about and whose opinion matters to you.

Next, write down what you think they'll think of you for trying this thing you want to try – it could even be their thoughts on you doing this 10-day challenge, because when you unlock your courage and start to unleash your self-belief, things are going to change in your life!

Now ask yourself: *Do I know that this is how they'll react, or am I just making it up?* Will your parents really be disappointed in you for trying something new and it not working out? Will your friends really laugh at you? Some of these things may be true, or none of them.

If you believe there's a chance that your worries may be real, write down how you can take ownership of your failures. There's no shame in trying something and it not working out – none whatsoever. And anyone who tries to make you feel that you've disappointed them in some way because of this needs to be reminded that the biggest failure of all isn't trying in the first place.

Ask yourself: *Why do I want or need their approval?* Write down the answer to this; it could be as simple as wanting their love or friendship.

Now think about whether you believe in what you're doing enough to carry on, regardless of whether or not you have their approval. This is a biggie, especially for women. We're raised to subconsciously seek approval for everything we do – firstly from our parents, then our teachers, friends, bosses and partners, even our children! Close your eyes and ask yourself: *Do I believe in what I'm doing, and will I do it even if those I love are disappointed in me?*

The answer to this should be yes. Even though that feels horrible, and horribly difficult. I'd say that this has been the most challenging part of my life's journey: learning how to do things that I know will cause disappointment in others. But once I learned to do it, I can't stress strongly enough how liberating it was. I wish I'd learned how to do it years ago – it would have saved me so much time!

Sit with this list and your responses to the questions for a while and go through it again. Imagine how it will feel to unlock your courage and go ahead anyway, regardless of others' reactions. Imagine how it will feel to have the courage and self-belief to do what feels right for you. It will feel *good*!

6. You're Afraid of Succeeding

This might seem like a pretty strange reason to be afraid to try something – surely that's the wrong way round? Not when you think about it logically. Look at how much flack 'successful' people receive. It starts with the way their own family and friends treat them; some view their success as shining a light on their own perceived failings and this causes jealousy, rifts, division – way more so than if everyone just stays in their lane.

Or how about the A-list actor who the newspapers have a field day with when their 'perfect' life is revealed to be the same as everyone else's – that is, with family fallouts, mistakes, dramas and tensions.

Look at elite sportspeople who are ripped apart because they 'only got a bronze' at the Olympics or missed a penalty in the final of a football tournament. These are people who have worked tirelessly for years with one aim in mind: to get to the very top of their field. And for what? Jealousy, ridicule, criticism?

You can see why it takes a special kind of dedication and focus to commit to wanting success: while the rewards are there for all to see, your family, friends, the public and the media are poised and waiting to see you fall from grace.

It's much easier to say it's the fear of getting it wrong that terrifies you rather than the fear of getting it right. The costs of true success are higher than most of us are willing to pay, yet there aren't many who will admit that this is what they're afraid of when they hold themselves back.

Walking Away

My life's been pretty much an open book in terms of when things have gone well for me and when things have fallen apart catastrophically, and I've felt I've let people down. I've accepted that this comes with doing a job in the public eye – for more than two decades I worked for a national broadcaster as a daytime TV presenter, spending 13 years as anchor of *Loose Women*, the UK version of the US show *The View*.

As I explained earlier, in December 2020, in the midst of the COVID-19 pandemic, I decided to make a life change. This wasn't a swift decision. It was one I'd been contemplating for a while – I'd just been waiting until the time felt *right*.

In the past two years, we've experienced fear on a worldwide scale as all our usual crutches have been kicked to the long grass by the pandemic and we've had to find new ways to stand tall. This has meant that as a global society we've had to rethink *everything* that we'd previously felt was right, wrong, normal or acceptable in our lives.

I came to the conclusion that while I loved working as a TV anchor, I needed to challenge myself to do something that felt right to *me*, as a person, not just as the breadwinner. Nick and I had been working hard on my website, thisgirlisonfire.com, for over two years, dedicating all our spare time to supporting women and helping them overcome their fears – him overseeing the logistics, me overseeing the content. And I decided I wanted to make this a full-time thing.

I knew that if I could overcome everything I'd done and experienced personally – abuse, divorce, single parenthood, being a working mother, a stepmother, a wife – and utilize my professional experience as an entrepreneur and communicator, my compassion, dedication and skill set would make a success of it.

To the outside world it didn't make much logical sense. I quit a very well-paid job to launch a brand-new personal growth membership business at a time when presenters, actors and performers were seeing their livelihood disappear with little hope of its return.

I had no other work – all my live event hosting and speaking gigs had vanished overnight when the pandemic hit. My agent thought I was insane and strongly advised against it. I took advice from the top PR firm in the UK, which also strongly advised against it. But it felt right *to me*.

Coming Out of Our Shell

Isn't this the reason why most of us stay silent and keep plodding on: because we're frightened that if we articulate what it is that deep down we *really* want, then we'll have to make changes to our lives? Those changes may not please those around us; they may mean a financial risk, and they may mean failure. And even more frightening, they may mean success. And then what will we do? If our wish actually comes true? Will we be able to cope?

You see, there are many reasons why we hold ourselves back from unlocking the courage we all have inside us, setting goals, making plans, saying them out loud and then putting them into action. We can decide in our own mind that 'this will be the year that I...' (insert whatever it is you want here, whether it's a lifestyle change, a health goal, a career move). That's the easy part.

The hard bit is sticking to it and putting in the graft when you've run out of enthusiasm, which is why most of us give up and decide we just aren't up to the work. Sometimes we use the excuse that we aren't brave enough, and we tuck our head back into our shell and hide away, feeling silent shame at our lack of stickability.

Or, if our venture genuinely hasn't worked out and we've had to walk away, we feel shame and embarrassment. But we shouldn't. We gave it a go. Take it from someone who knows, who hasn't just been there but is still there. Still trying, every single day, to make things work – for my family, my relationship and my business.

Life isn't a movie or a novel or a witty article in which a montage of all your best bits is summed up with a pithy headline.

Life really sucks sometimes, and while staying hidden away in your shell makes it a less scary place to be, it doesn't make it any safer. A turtle hiding in his shell on the beach because he's too scared to swim in the sea can still get swooped up by a bird.

You only get one life, so you may as well live it doing something that scares you a little, because it could also bring you unimaginable happiness.

Journal Time ✍

So today, I'd like you to ask yourself: *What three things would I attempt to do if I knew I couldn't fail?* If none of the fears we've just talked about existed, what would you do?

Write those three things in your journal. Then underneath them, write down honestly what it is that's stopping you from doing these three things: which fear is stopping you?

This may take a while. Don't worry if nothing comes to mind right away – you can mull this over all day if you like. But by the end of today, make sure you've written down at least one thing that you'd attempt to do if you weren't afraid.

Figuring Out What You Want

You may think that because you're reading a book about unlocking your courage and reclaiming your power it's going to be all about how to kick ass, be the best, be the boss – be a success! And you'd be partly right; however, this is only a tiny fraction of what being brave is.

Most of our ingrained definitions of success have been sold to us by people who either want us to work ourselves to death for their gain or buy stuff that we don't need to make them more successful.

> **True success is living a life you love – one that works for you, one that challenges you in ways that help you grow rather than breaking you.**

In this section, we'll be digging into *why* you're feeling the way you do right now, as well as looking at the possibilities for change that are available to you and how you'll reward yourself for successfully making them!

You see, being successful isn't about having one huge goal that's years away – it's about smaller goals that you hit along the way, taking the time to pat yourself on the back and *reward yourself* for doing so well!

The main reason so many of us are afraid of success is because we don't feel valued or feel that we deserve it. And that's because we're waiting for *other people* to value what we're doing. You need to put a value *on yourself* and have your own way of checking off when you're succeeding in getting what you want.

Another reason many people feel unsuccessful is because they don't know what they want, in any part of their life, which means they never get it. If this is you, by that reasoning, you'll always have a niggling feeling that things aren't quite right, that you've failed in some way. You'll never have a successful life if you don't know what you want from it – which seems like such a wasted opportunity, don't you think?

So, let's help you figure out what you want and how you can get it, beginning with something called the Circle of Life.

Your Circle of Life Challenge

Other than being an epic song from *The Lion King*, the Circle of Life (also known as the Wheel of Life) is a powerful tool for assessing how you're living right now and whether things are flowing in the way they should. It's a starting point for making changes because it allows you to see how balanced (or not) your life is in this moment.

The Circle of Life is particularly useful if you're in denial about things – which let's be honest, most of us are – because it enables you to see the areas of your life that are coming up short.

And why do these areas come up short? Because we're too afraid to make the changes necessary to the things that cause us the most stress or unhappiness – whether that takes the form of refusing to look at bank statements or deal with debt, or accepting that we need to have some difficult conversations about our relationship. So, we ignore them and hope they'll change by themselves. Which they never will.

There are eight segments in the Circle of Life, and each one represents an area of life:

♦ Personal Development

♦ Health and Fitness

♦ Finance

♦ Family and Friends

♦ Spirituality

♦ Business and Career

♦ Fun and Recreation

♦ Romance and Relationships

Using the example opposite as a guide, I'd like you to complete a Circle of Life in your journal/notebook. First, draw the Circle itself and divide it into eight segments; then label each segment with a life area, as shown.

Next, consider each of those eight life areas on your Circle in turn and give it a score of between 1 and 10 based on your current

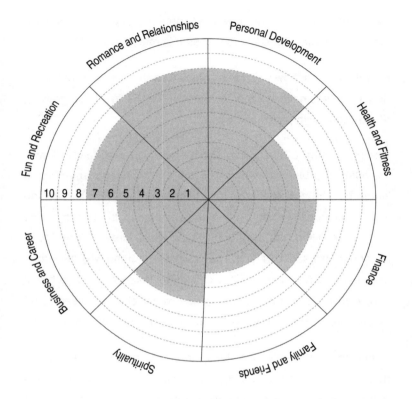

The Circle of Life

level of satisfaction with it; in other words, how you feel *right now* – with 0 being very dissatisfied and 10 being very satisfied.

Now, 'fill in' your score for each life area, as shown on the example. Once you've scored each area on the Circle, you'll have a visual snapshot of the aspects of your life that are flourishing right now and those that need improvement.

Next, write down *why* you gave the scores that you did for each life area in your Circle of Life. How does this make you feel?

Now think about how you'd *like* to feel in each life area. What score do you *want* to have in each area of your life? Fill in a fresh drawing of the Circle with *those* scores.

Completing the Circle of Life should help you see, really clearly, the difference between where you are right now and where you'd like to be. Don't worry about this difference right now: just seeing it is a very positive step. So many people go through their life feeling unfulfilled, but they don't know which area of their life is leading to this sense of lack. They can't understand why they don't feel successful. But during this challenge, *you* are going to break things down so that it's simple to see where changes need to be made – and how you can feel successful in *every* area of your life!

Doing this challenge will take time, so give yourself some headspace to draw and complete your Circle of Life and then respond to the associated questions below. I'd encourage you to bookmark this page, as hopefully, you'll come back to the Circle later and recomplete it. It's a really great way to keep track of how you're doing.

Building a Successful Life

Now, most of the time when we think about success, we'll only consider the Business and Career and the Finance segments of the Circle of Life, but there's much more to our life than that. So, why would we omit things like Romance and Relationships or

Family and Friends? Why do we wish so hard to have a wonderful partner and great kids and then never do anything about spending quality time nurturing them?

By this, I don't mean 'looking after them' – I mean enjoyable time spent relaxing with each other. Because it's good to get everyone involved with this challenge, not just you. It's impossible to make any kind of significant change to your environment on your own: you need to get your team on board!

The best way to do that is to see this as a challenge where everyone benefits. It will also help everyone understand where they are in life right now – you'll understand why your partner wants time to meet friends, and he or she will understand why you need some 'couple time' or 'gym time' or 'leave me the hell alone time'.

So, once you've completed this challenge yourself and feel comfortable sharing the idea with your partner and family, get them to fill in their Circle of Life, and open up the discussion about how they'd like to change their scores.

Business and Career

Let's get straight to the point: if you don't work right now and don't plan to, then you can skip this section as it'll waste your time. If you're not working right now but you want to be working, then you'll find this useful. If you're working right now but want to make some changes (either to move job or to make things more enjoyable in the one you're in), then you'll find this useful.

The following questions are simple, but they'll make you think about what you're doing right now and why you're doing it. Remember, though: there's no such thing as a 'perfect job'. All jobs involve times that are challenging, stressful or boring, so if you're hoping to find the perfect job then I'm afraid I'll have to burst your bubble.

Being successful professionally isn't about having an easy time of things and being paid loads of money – it's about getting the balance right between work that stimulates you, challenges you and rewards you emotionally, and work that rewards you financially.

Write down the answers to these questions in your journal under the heading Business and Career:

◆ What do you do for a living?

◆ Do you enjoy it?

◆ Why did you choose to do the job you do?

◆ Which parts of your job do you love?

◆ What would you change about your job if you could?

◆ How could you make those changes?

◆ If you can't make those changes within your current job, what steps can you take to change your job – either within your current workplace or in a new company?

◆ Who can you speak to about making these changes happen?

♦ Where can you find useful information to help you make these changes?

♦ Which three things are you going to do to start making those changes?

♦ How will you reward yourself for making those changes?

♦ How will you reward yourself when all those changes are made?

Congratulations! You've now figured out what it is about your job that's either holding you back or making you unhappy, and you've outlined a plan of action to make the changes necessary to get to where you want to be. And importantly, you know how you're going to *reward* yourself for this. It's the rewarding ourselves for reaching our goals that tells us we've succeeded in doing something well, and that's a key part of helping us feel successful.

Personal Development

This section can be about any area of your life that concerns *you*. This will be a mixture of all the parts of your life that mean something to you. It will help you work out which areas need a bit of tweaking or attention and how to go about doing that.

These are really useful questions to ask yourself about one area of your life at a time, rather than trying to squash your whole life in together. Write down the answers in your journal under the heading Personal Development.

- ◆ How are you feeling about life right now?

- ◆ Did you choose the life you're living right now, or did you just find yourself here?

- ◆ Which parts of your life do you love?

- ◆ What would you change about your life if you could?

- ◆ How could you make those changes?

- ◆ Can you make those changes by yourself?

- ◆ If you need help with this, who can you speak to, to make these changes happen?

- ◆ Where can you find information to help you make these changes?

- ◆ Which three things will you do to start making those changes?

- ◆ How will you reward yourself for making those changes?

Congratulations! You've now figured out which parts of your life aren't working for you right now and have outlined a plan of action to make the changes necessary to get to where you want to be. And importantly, you know how you're going to *reward* yourself for this, in every part of your life. This means that you'll have a lot of rewards coming your way, all earned by you and delivered by you. You're not waiting for anyone else to value what you've done to make these changes; you're placing value on yourself and rewarding yourself for doing so well!

Romance and Relationships

Okay, you're probably thinking it so I'll say it for you: 'How can I take relationship advice from someone who's been married *three times*?'

My answer is this: would you take swimming lessons from someone who's never been in a pool? Would you accept cookery tips from someone who wouldn't know a saucepan if it hit them in the face? No, you wouldn't. Like every single part of our lives, the only way we learn what works for us is by learning what doesn't.

When it comes to relationships there's fantastic advice to be had from couples who've been together since their teens and are still in love 70 years on. Much of it will be the same as what I'll talk about here because a successful romantic relationship is one that involves learning, compromise, shared experiences and growth.

You can learn just as much about what does or doesn't work for you from someone who's only seen the inside of a solid relationship as you can from the perspective of someone who's experienced a fractured one. I now (and it's taken time to get to this point!) consider myself fortunate to have experienced both.

However, most of the time, the real questions that need answering are the ones we must ask ourselves. Others can offer a different perspective and experience to help you think about your own situation, but ultimately, the success or otherwise of your relationship happens because of how *you* experience it, no one else.

Some of these things can be done on your own, but for a relationship to be successful, both parties need to be invested in its success, at whatever level works for them. This isn't about creating a fairy tale – it's about nurturing something that you and your partner care about, in your own unique way.

Let's begin; again, write down your responses in your notebook/ journal, under the heading Romance and Relationships.

◆ How are feeling about your relationship right now?

◆ Did you choose the kind of relationship you're having right now, or did you just find yourself here, with no real idea how it worked out like this?

◆ Which parts of your relationship do you love?

◆ Without assigning fault or blame, what would you change about your relationship if you could? Think of this in a positive light: that you'd love it if *this* happened, rather than you hate it when *that* happens.

◆ Can you make those changes by yourself?

◆ How receptive is your partner to making these changes?

◆ If you need help with this, who can you speak to outside of your relationship, to make these changes happen?

◆ Where can you find information to help you make these changes?

♦ Which three things will you do to start making those changes?

♦ How will you reward yourself for making those changes?

Well done – the Romance and Relationships exercise was the most difficult part of this section as it involves someone else's feelings and views on how your relationship is doing, and this can be a challenging conversation to have. So, congratulate yourself for completing it.

Balancing the Circle

I hope you can now see that much of your fear of success lies in your own hands. It isn't simply about having a fabulous job or loads of cash – it's about keeping an eye on all areas of your life, so that your Circle of Life is in a balanced state.

Working on all these areas, keeping an eye on them, doing little things every day that keep us on the right path, remembering to reward ourselves for having done so – *that's* when we're successful, because we've unlocked our courage and reclaimed our power in a way that feels natural and right for us. And there's nothing to be afraid of when it comes to that.

Once you've completed this book and started implementing the changes you want to make, come back to your Circle of Life and fill it in again. Do this regularly to keep an eye on how you're doing and to remind yourself why you're doing it. Why do it? Because *you love yourself* and you know that you're worthy of living a successful life that works for you. *You just need to believe it.*

Well done! This Circle of Life challenge took a lot of time and effort, and you may have found yourself digging around in parts of your life that haven't had much attention for a while, either because you've forgotten to look at them or because they've been too painful to look at. Doing all this takes courage, and I hope you're starting to see that you have much more of it inside you than you realized!

***

Tomorrow we're going to be looking at our fears and learning how to face them head on. We all have things that we're afraid of, that trigger old emotions of vulnerability and make us shy away from taking any kind of bold action. Now that you know what you'd attempt to do if you knew you couldn't fail, let's look at those fears with love, compassion and the iron will to get them onside.

Remember the tiger pacing outside your cage? Tomorrow we look her in the face and show her that *we* are the ones in charge. By the end of the day, she'll be walking by your side, defending you rather than defeating you.

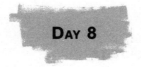

DAY 8

Tame Your Fear Trigger

*'Feel it. The thing you don't want to
feel. Feel it and be free.'*

NAYYIRAH WAHEED

What are you *really* afraid of? If you had to dig down, deeper than you did yesterday, so that you aren't just looking at things you think you might mess up, get wrong or embarrass yourself with. What's *really* eating you up? I bet you don't even know. It's hard to put a name to something that you can't nail down. Is it a single thing, or a collection of many? Or is it as simple as not wanting to feel uncomfortable?

Discomfort comes to us in many forms, but we tend to focus on the physicality of it. I don't like being cold, so I won't go for a walk if it's raining and miserable outside. Short of moving to a hot country, it's not something I can stay away from permanently, but I certainly do my best to skirt around it! This may seem like a lame comparison when it comes to the thornier elements of fear and what triggers us mentally rather than physically – but hear me out.

Unlocking My Courage

In October 2018, when I was 49 years old, I took part in a reality TV show called *SAS: Who Dares Wins*. At the time, I was the oldest person ever to take part (they've since lowered the application age to 44) and it was the first time they had accepted women. If you haven't seen the show, the premise is brutally simple: a selection of 'recruits' are put through a version of the vigorous training undertaken by the SAS elite, involving mental and physical extremes in both behaviour and endurance. Brutal. Simple.

Why did I decide to take part? Because I wanted to see what I was capable of when someone else set the bar for my discomfort. That may sound like an odd reason, but I was curious to see how far from the comforts of my normal surroundings I could push myself, including being forced into situations I'd never normally allow myself to be in because they frightened me.

To some, it seemed like a very strange decision; after all, I'd already survived an abusive relationship, divorce, single parenting, money worries and physical illness. Why would I want to put myself through an experience where the only guarantee was physical and mental pain? It's a very good question and the answer is twofold: I didn't know exactly what would happen to me, and I wanted to know where my line in the sand was.

I appreciate that this was an extreme way of finding out, but it was an opportunity that came my way and I believe that it did so for a reason. There were many moments of intense mental and physical discomfort during my time on the show, but the one I'm going to describe now is the one that's most important to me. If you've read my book *This Girl Is On Fire*, you'll know how difficult my SAS experience was, but this is the moment when for me, everything came together. I just didn't know it at the time.

Walking off a Cliff

It was some time in the afternoon – I didn't know when exactly because our watches and phones had been taken off us when we'd arrived, along with all our other possessions. The sky was darkening, as much from the storm clouds that were roaring towards us as the ending day. The wind had arrived first, then the sleet, stinging my face with wet ice.

I was standing near the edge of a cliff face somewhere in the Andes Mountains in Chile, waiting quietly as the SAS officer clicked and checked my harness and ropes. I'd been ordered to go next because it was becoming clear that something was seriously wrong with me. The storm was approaching faster than anyone had anticipated, and the cold had now got into my bones.

I'd rationalized this as we'd sat in a huddle, my brain surprisingly calm and clear despite the debilitating cold and altitude. It's when you stop shaking that you have to worry, I'd been told – that's when the hypothermia gets you. I wasn't quite there yet; I was at the convulsing stage, somewhere past delicate shivering and just before keeling over.

I categorized my thoughts: a) I was not well, and I needed to get off this mountain; b) there was no other way off than doing it myself. Thinking about it logically calmed me down: 'This is the problem. That is the solution. Do that.'

I listened as the officer shouted instructions over the noise of the wind. He held the back of my harness as I inched my way towards the edge of the cliff. I gripped my rope tightly in my right hand; this was my brake.

'Lean forwards!' he shouted. 'Keep your body straight! Lean out! Out!'

My fearful brain roared at me: 'Forwards? Into the air? Is he *mad*?' I stumbled as fear tried to swipe my legs from under me, to stop me from doing such an obviously stupid, dangerous thing.

'Again! Keep straight! Lean forwards!' My logical brain spoke up: *The longer you take, the longer you're up here.*

I pushed my feet to the furthest point of the cliff and then looked out, tentatively testing my weight against the rope attached to my harness. I could feel the tension as it began to take the strain. I pulled my right arm out to the side, testing the braking action of this rope that was capable of letting me go and pulling me back all at once.

'Forwards!' I looked straight ahead, forcing my brain not to think about the consequences of getting this wrong. I forced my body to lean into the wide Chilean sky, now unable to see or hear anyone else as the wind stung my eyes into slits and battered my ears. My toes clutched at the rockface through my boots, curling into my socks in a futile attempt to pull me back to safety.

'Forwards.' I was at a 90° angle to the cliff face now, staring down. The wall was now my floor. All I had to do was release my brake and walk.

My fear had become a living entity. It wasn't so much an emotion as a beast that was roaring inside me, battering itself against the cage of my body, screaming at me to stop. I could feel it pummelling my heart and rattling my kneecaps. I could hear the rush of it in my chest and head. There were two of us on this rope: me and the beast that was my fear – and one of them needed to shut the fuck up so the other could get off the fucking mountain.

I leaned directly into my fear of falling, of pain, of death. I looked into her eyes; I held her face in my hands and breathed slowly, in and out. The tiger looked back at me and then stepped off my chest, allowing me to pass.

I released the brake and took my first step.

'Keep. Going.'

Step.

'Keep. Going.'

Step.

I didn't realize that I'd been saying this out loud, all the way down the cliff face, until I got to the bottom and the SAS officer waiting for me there grinned and said: 'You can stop now. You're here. Well bloody done.'

Moments later, I was falling to the ground and being half-carried to the waiting ambulance. They were right: it's when you stop shaking that you have to worry. That's when the hypothermia got me. *But that was also the moment that I unlocked my courage and reclaimed my power.*

Looking Fear in the Face

My time on the show ended that day, but for me it was the start of looking at my life in a completely different way. I knew that I'd been brave in the face of difficult moments before, but I now saw that I'd faced them through an instinctive reaction, rather than understanding the logic behind what I was feeling and doing.

Since that time, I've devoted myself to this learning, so I can understand more about how the human mind works, what makes us tick and how we can utilize our innate ability to cope with stress and discomfort in a way that works best for us at *all* times, not just in stressful times.

Trying to live a life without fear or discomfort is impossible. Even if you locked yourself away in the most beautiful room, surviving on room service pushed under your door, with endless Netflix, a masseuse on call and a guard at your door so nothing scary or uncomfortable was allowed in, *it would still find you.* How?

> Most of what we're afraid of lives
> inside our head, so no matter how
> much we lock ourselves away, we
> can't escape from ourselves.

Feeling overwhelmed with fear and discomfort isn't new, but today it's called, among other things, 'triggering'. Unfortunately, this term is also sometimes used to label anything that features uncomfortable components of the human condition, which can make it difficult to know whether you're about to witness something extremely upsetting or something many of us would see as a normal part of life. This labelling, which is helpful and useful when applied where it's genuinely needed, can be confusing and unhelpful when applied to everything we see, do and experience.

The Value of Suffering

In his book *The Importance of Suffering: The Value and Meaning of Emotional Discontent*, Dr James Davies, a psychotherapist and reader in social anthropology and mental health at the UK's University of Roehampton, examines the value of suffering as part of the human experience. It is, he explains, something that should be seen as part and parcel of how we develop and learn as humans, rather than something to be avoided through fear or anaesthetized via medication, illegal drugs or alcohol.[1]

That may seem extreme, but if we step back and look at how we personally behave around things we find painful or uncomfortable, we'll see that avoidance or numbing are usually our first call. Suffering is, as Dr Davies says, normally a sign that there are things in our lives we should be changing rather than avoiding or numbing, and in making this change we can transform our lives in incredibly powerful ways. In fact, he claims, denying ourselves suffering means denying ourselves the 'fruits of discontent... positive transformation'.[2]

James Davies isn't the only professional in his field who's concerned that we're now so afraid to see, hear or feel things that make us uncomfortable that we're as afraid of the *idea* of the discomfort as we are of the thing itself that makes us uncomfortable. It's something that I can understand and see both sides of – discomfort and fear are horrible experiences so why would we want to experience them if there was a way to avoid them?

To put this into context, Davies makes it clear that he isn't talking about extreme trauma or medical conditions, which of course need care and attention – and nor am I. In this book, and in this context, I'm talking about the experiences that make up the normal light and shade of the human condition; I'm not devaluing the trauma that causes triggering in its rawest, most vulnerable sense.

I've used Dr Davies' example to show that it's possible – and indeed, we're positively encouraged in this – to look our fears in the face in order to overcome them. And that simply walking in a different direction from our fears in a bid to avoid them, or numbing our feelings around them, or demanding that the rest of the world stops doing things in front of us which we personally find unacceptable, means they'll always be in control of us.

This takes courage, I know, but (and again, I stress that I'm talking about everyday things that may have become overwhelming for us, not events and medical conditions that require professional help) our fears can be overcome.

In the Introduction, I used the analogy of fear as a tiger that roars to protect us from things that have the potential to hurt us. That fear can be reasoned with, harnessed and use for good.

'Trigger the Dog'

When it comes to being triggered by our fears it helps to visualize them in a way that makes them less frightening to us. As we've just discussed, those fears will always be there and expecting the rest of the world to change so that we aren't affected by them is unrealistic, and hiding from them also doesn't work.

If the analogy of fear as a tiger seems too overbearing for your worries, perhaps it may help you to imagine them as a scary dog that you're frightened to walk towards. Unless you find a way to face the dog and stare it down, you'll end up locked in your home, too scared to leave in case you encounter it. Worse still, very often that scary dog lives in your own head, so it will find its way past any locked door or guard.

I find the 'fear as a dog' analogy useful because anyone who's ever come face to face with a frightening dog knows that it's snarly because it knows you're afraid of it. The most powerful thing you can do to get it to back away is to stop being afraid of it.

This is almost impossible to do because every part of you is screaming in terror! And yet, forcing yourself to take deep breaths that slow your racing heart and help keep you calm, will have an effect on the dog. It calms down because you calm down. And you're able to pass it and carry on with your day.

If it helps you to visualize your fear as a big scary dog that you need to face, take this one step further and imagine that it's called 'Trigger'. Rather than instantly latching on to the notion of something 'triggering' you, call the thing itself by that name. Imagine it as the dog. Imagine facing that scary dog called Trigger and know that if you want to, you have the power to make him sit, and then lie down, and then roll over and play dead. All by acknowledging your fear and taking action to calm it.

You'll *never* be able to control everything in the world that's your personal 'Trigger the dog'. You can't make every dog stop being a dog just because you find them scary. But you can control how you react to them. And that in itself will make them less frightening, until your personal Trigger becomes just a dog you must pass, and you barely notice one other. The dog will still be there. You'll still be there. But how you experience him will change.

Your Tame Your Fear Triggers Challenge

Finding out what our triggers are is tricky because we don't always recognize them. I know that mine are being betrayed by friends and abused by lovers – both things that I've experienced. I react very badly to anger or being patronized. I feel conflicted, partly fearful, and I can automatically shrink, acquiesce and go quiet.

But I also feel rage at these feelings: I fight back and keep fighting back because I refuse to return to that place where I feel small again. I roar. I don't always get it right, and I can roar when a quiet word would have sufficed. It happens. I'm human, and I make mistakes. We all are, and we all do.

We all have our triggers. For some of us, they stem from a childhood in which we never felt good enough. For others, they stem from a friend, partner or colleague who constantly belittles us and makes us afraid to try. Whatever yours are, remember that you're not alone in feeling this way. The trick is to have an answer ready for when these triggers pop up (which they always will), even if it's just to shut down your own negative thoughts.

Journal Time ✍

Remember Trigger the dog. The way to deal with him is to calm your breathing, slow down your racing heart and let your mind return to its normal, clearer thinking. If your trigger has found its way into your head and is snarling untruths in your ear, remember that you're the one in control. You have the power to tame it.

Try this:

Replace	With
'You're pathetic.'	'I'm trying my best.'
'You're ugly.'	'I'm beautiful/handsome.'
'Why are you even bothering?'	'I'm worth spending time on.'
'It's not going to work.'	'It might just work.'
'It's not worth the effort.'	'I'm worth the effort.'
'It's going to fail.'	'I'm going to learn something along the way.'
'You're making a fool of yourself.'	'I'm prepared to – it's how I grow.'
'You're an embarrassment.'	'I'm unique.'
'You don't even know what you're doing.'	'Not yet, but I'm learning.'
'What if I lose everything?'	'I'll start all over again.'
'What if no one likes it?'	'I'll keep trying until I succeed.'
'What if I can't do it?'	'I'll learn how.'
'What if I fail?'	*'What if I fly?'*

In your journal, write down your thoughts about these phrases. How will it feel to replace the negative, fearful and unhelpful phrases with positive, uplifting ones?

Think about a time in your life – either something you're living through right now or problems you foresee in the future because of the changes you're making – and counterbalance your fear triggers with words of courage and reassurance.

Doing this every day will normalize these thoughts, so that when fear growls (which it will always do) you'll be ready for it with words that remind you of just how incredible and courageous you really are.

. . . .

Well done for getting through today. I know it's been a pretty uncomfortable experience for you, and I hope that you've managed to uncover some helpful learnings that will calm your racing mind the next time something happens to you or around you that would normally send you into a tailspin of negative emotions.

Remember: you're your thoughts. You're not your fears. You're not your feelings. They're just what you're experiencing right now, at this moment in time. With the Unlock Your Courage visualization in the Introduction and the meditation guidance in Day 6, you now have the tools you need to calm down those thoughts, calm down your body, calm down your mind. *You* are in control. You have the courage you need within you. *You just need to believe it.*

Tomorrow we're going to look at the power of moving our body to get rid of the fear and negativity that weighs us down and holds us back. We're going to start gearing up to celebrate – because you're almost there!

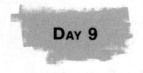

DAY 9

Let's Get Moving!

'No matter how slow you go, you're still
lapping everyone on the couch.'

ANONYMOUS

Let's shake things up a little now! Over the past eight days, you've worked really hard at changing your focus, setting yourself the task of forming new habits and opening yourself up to the rawness of accepting yourself as you are.

This is where the process of unlocking your courage begins. It doesn't come from an outside source. It doesn't come through force. It comes from *inside*, from changing how you see yourself and the challenges you're facing. It comes from shifting your perspective and your energy – no one feels as if they can take on the world if they're feeling flat, heavy-hearted, squashed by the darkness and enormity of their problems.

The 10 Ways in 10 Days process won't take away your difficulties – when you reach the end of it, they'll still be there! But *you* will have changed. You will be looking at them differently: through opened eyes, a full heart and in an energized state.

Moving Makes You Feel Good

Being energized plays a huge part in changing your life. There's a reason why people who move their bodies look and seem so different to those who barely move from the sofa all day. They have more energy, and they want to do more – to try new things, to push themselves further in every part of their life, not just physically.

Don't worry, this isn't the part where I tell you to sign up to run a marathon or climb a mountain – but if you did, I'd be cheering you on all the way! But it *is* the part where I'm going to encourage you to start moving your body more.

Committing to making any kind of change in your life is scary and uncomfortable, I know that. But hopefully by now you'll have seen and started to experience for yourself the benefits of looking that discomfort in the face and saying *you don't scare me.*

Physical activity is a way of turning up the volume on all those positive feelings, and not simply because it makes you feel so damn good. It's been scientifically proven that when we feel depressed, we move more slowly; we 'feel heavier', physically, than we do when we feel mentally strong and positive. It makes it even more difficult to get up and move about, even though we know it's good for us, because the body feels incapable and the mind is unwilling.

Telling someone that they just need to get up and move isn't helpful – as anyone who's been on the receiving end of this advice knows only too well. What's useful to know, however, is that our brain and body are so in tune (of course they are!) that movement of any kind can be enough to kick-start the endorphins we all need to get our mind feeling uplifted and energized. It's as simple as changing your state.

This doesn't have to mean feeling the burn at the gym or thrashing around in a class. You may be relieved to hear this! It can be as simple as standing up and stretching. Rotating your arms and listening to them clunk and click. Rotating your wrists. Swaying your hips from side to side. Bending forwards and then slowly standing up straight. All of these are great places to start because you're moving! Remember to breathe deeply in and out as well – most of the time we aren't getting enough oxygen into our bodies, which is why we feel so tired.

Movement and Mood

During the pandemic, when we were forced to stay indoors and were only allowed out for an hour a day to exercise, the streets and parks of Britain were filled with people going for their daily walks. Some of them looked bewildered as they blinked in the sunshine; perhaps they were thinking, *I didn't even know I had a local park. Where have all these trees come from?* Some people took up running, cycling or online fitness classes for the very first time, purely to keep their bodies moving and give them something to do.

However, according to a Harvard medical paper by Dr Srini Pillay, the way you move can affect the way you think and feel. Doing something as simple as going for a walk can give you what's known as a 'back door' to the mental changes you need, without having to 'psych yourself into feeling better'.[1] Dr Pillay says that regular exercise can be as effective as medication and psychotherapy, helping improve mood by increasing a brain protein that helps nerve fibres to grow.

And the UK mental health charity Mind tells us that physical activity can help improve sleep and manage stress, anxiety or intrusive and racing thoughts.[2] It can also boost your self-esteem and confidence by making you feel good, especially if you join a group activity and meet new people. If exercise or regular movement of some kind isn't part of your daily routine, I'd strongly urge you to look into making it so.

Get Your Playlist On

The first place I'd like you to go is the free playlist I've made especially for you. You can find it on Spotify: search for You Just Need to Believe It. If you can't blast these songs out at full volume in your home, stick in those headphones and crank up the volume! (To a safe level, of course: you've gotta take care of those ears.)

I guarantee that within a couple of tunes you won't be able to keep still – you'll feel *charged up* and ready to take on the world! *That* is the power of music. That is the power of *you* set to music. I know first-hand what a difference listening to a great playlist makes.

I've got through many a dull commute by listening to my favourite tunes. But moving to music? That's a whole different ball game.

When I first created this 10-day challenge, I had the chance to speak with some of the people who took part in it and hearing their stories of transformation literally made my heart soar with pride – they were incredible.

But the story that really stuck in my head was from a young woman, a mum to two little children, who'd been struggling with her mental health; it was the middle of the pandemic and she'd barely been able to leave the house to get some fresh air, never mind some peace. Then she remembered the playlist I'd created as part of the challenge, and she put it on, as loud as she could, and started dancing around the kitchen.

The kids were giggling, she said – they couldn't take their eyes off her. She danced and danced and danced until she was red-faced and out of breath. Her eyes shining with happiness, she told me it had totally changed her day. She'd been stressed and could feel a panic attack coming on – that was made worse by the fact that she couldn't get out the house and the kids were climbing the walls. For 20 minutes or so, she forgot all that, and by moving her body she changed her state, mentally as well as physically. It works!

Which Type of Exercise Best Suits You?

So, what exercise will *you* commit to, to help you stay on track with your mental growth, unlock your courage and truly believe that you can make the positive changes to your life that you've always wanted to make but were too afraid to? I'm a huge believer in exercise as a tool for both our physical and mental wellbeing – after all, I run a membership that's all about being a 'gym for the mind'! As far as I'm concerned, the two go hand in hand.

However, if you've not done any kind of activity for a while, it's not a good idea to hit the ground running. You may hurt yourself physically, and mentally you'll feel demoralized, which won't do you any good at all. You could start by simply having a dance around the house, running up and down the stairs, playing an active computer game – there are quite a few that involve doing exercises in front of a screen, including things like tennis and bowling.

If you're not quite ready to go to a gym, you can start building up your energy and confidence by doing online classes, so you get used to it. Once you're ready to get out and about, join a local club or team, especially if it's something you've always liked the idea of trying but felt too shy or not good enough. Join anyway! Your local leisure centre will have lots of classes to choose from, for people of all levels. Here are some other ideas.

Yoga

The benefits of yoga are far-reaching, long-lasting and multifaceted. First of all, everyone can do it – it's why they send yoga teachers into nursing homes to help the residents bend and stretch. You don't need anything special to do it, and you can do it anywhere. Yoga helps lower stress levels, boosts your immune system and calms your mind, as well as making your body feel great.

I've done yoga for years, which means you probably think I'm one of these people who can fold herself into a tiny ball like a Cirque de Soleil performer. Nope. Every single day when I get up it's like Groundhog Day, where my body forgets that it stretched the day before and has overnight reverted into its natural rusty robot level of stiffness. I can barely bend over, let alone touch my toes or do a downward dog.

Everything hurts and there's much clicking and groaning as I try to tease my body into something resembling a sun salutation. So why bother? Because I feel so much better afterwards. I feel stretched and stronger. My back doesn't hurt as much. My neck doesn't feel as cricked. But the main benefits are in my head. Nothing helps me calm down and focus on something other than my whirring, anxious brain like yoga does.

Yoga starts with the breath – the deep breathing in and out sends oxygen to parts of me I didn't know were lacking it, and I instantly feel better. Focusing on my breath as I stumble about on my mat, trying not to fall over, stills my mind; I can almost go into a trance-like state once I get into the flow of it, moving in time to my breath: in, out, up, down. It feels beautiful. I've no idea what it looks like, and I don't care: it feels divine.

**Yoga is something that's practised,
which means there's no finish line with
it and there's no competition.**

Even if I go to a class, I know that there will be people there who are much more flexible or stronger than me, but it doesn't matter because I'm doing what I can, pushing to my limits to benefit *me*. And most of the time I have my eyes closed anyway, so I don't even look at what anyone else is doing.

If you'd like to give yoga a try, here are a couple of online teachers I'd recommend:

♦ **Yoga with Adriene**; www.yogawithadriene.com. Adriene seems like a beautiful soul, everything you want from a yoga teacher. And she does classes in her home, with her dog Benji usually wandering around, sometimes flopping onto the mat next to her. The classes are as simple or as difficult as you need them to be.

♦ **Asana Rebel** is an app that I like to use. It has a selection of 25-minute sessions, all beautifully filmed in lovely locations with soothing voiceovers and music. You can find it in the App Store.

♦ **Travis Eliot**; www.flexibilityandbeyond.com. Travis has a lovely energy, and his classes are great if you already have a good level of yoga experience.

Running

Why running? you might ask. Well, apart from the physical health benefits of increasing our cardio fitness, running helps us live longer, sleep better and have stronger joints. It also boosts immunity and reportedly improves cognitive function (we think faster and more clearly), reduces mild depression by boosting our mood and builds our self-esteem. Awesome!

I'm not a natural runner; I'm a slow runner who tries to go too fast and always ends up hurting herself. I hate how everything hurts. I do everything I can to procrastinate when it comes to going for a run, and sometimes I hate every single stride I take while I'm doing it. But I like how it makes me feel afterwards – when I'm back home, when my heart slows down; when I realize how far I managed to go, and I feel like I've pushed myself. Even if I've hated the experience, I *always* feel better after I've done it.

There are many local running clubs that I could have joined, but I prefer to do something like this on my own. However, you may like to join a running group and get motivated by everyone around you.

To get myself started again after a very long hiatus, I started a Couch to 5K running plan for beginners. There are many apps for this, but I used the BBC one: it's easy to find in the App Store and is free. I listened to the radio DJ Jo Whiley talking me through it, which really helped me feel less stupid about being so bad at it. You can also try the Couch to 5K Runner app, which has helped millions of people around the world get moving.

After a few months of plodding along at a ridiculously slow pace, I hit my 5K mark. Setting myself this goal, keeping to the plan the app set out for me and doing it even when I didn't feel like it, meant that on the day I completed it I felt as proud as a primary school child getting a medal on sports day!

Even though I was on my own and it's a pre-recorded app that has no idea whether I'm doing it or not, it made me feel *great!* So much so that I signed up for a 10K app and have just completed that! I've got my head around the fact that it's not a race, it's not about speed, and all I need to do is keep going – a metaphor for my life!

If you're interested in running – after all, you can do it whenever and wherever you like and you don't need to be a member of a club – then maybe you'd like to try for a *gasp* marathon. There are some great books out there that will talk you through the steps (no pun intended) that you need to take to build up to the full 26 miles. These include: *119 Days to Go: How to Train for and Run Your First Marathon* by Chris Evans and *Running Up That Hill: The Highs and Lows of Going That Bit Further* by Vassos Alexander.

Strength Training

Strength training is one of the best forms of low-impact cardio exercise. You might not think that standing in one place lifting weights will get your blood pumping but ask anyone who's swung a kettle bell whether they're getting a hard workout and the answer will be a resounding yes! It's the same with squats, lunges and press-ups – they get your heart pumping while strengthening your joints, building muscle and improving your mood and mental wellbeing. What's not to like?

> **The great thing about strength training is that you don't even need to leave the house to give it a try.**

This is great news if, say, you're a bit freaked out at the idea of entering the muscle men area of the gym. You can find resistance bands and weights online if there are no sports shops near you, and there are plenty of online tutorials to get you started.

One of the most popular women online right now for her strength training routines is Senada Greca. She works with resistance bands, dumbbells and body weight, for all levels. Her routines are pre-recorded and can be done at home or in a gym. Find her at www.senadagreca.com.

One of the most inspiring women I've ever seen in terms of changing attitudes to fitness is Joan MacDonald. At the time of writing, Joan is 73, and just three years ago she was struggling with high blood pressure and arthritis. She was feeling tired and emotional and lacked motivation in any part of her life. Then, encouraged by her daughter's love of fitness, she started training alongside her and is now stronger than women half her age! I love following Joan on Instagram to see what she's up to. She's the absolute epitome of *you just need to believe it!* Find her at www.trainwithjoanofficial.com.

Dance

It's no secret that me and synchronized movement are not happy bedfellows. I like to think that I'm too free-spirited to follow any kind of instruction, but the truth is that I just can't *remember* any kind of instruction. It goes right out of my head; I forget my left and right, and it all goes to pot.

The only kind of synchronized dance that I can do is salsa, which I love. I think it's because you only need a few basic steps and then you can make it your own. Dancing to amazing music and drinking rum at the same time. What's not to love?!

I got Nick to come with me to salsa classes shortly before the pandemic and it was a lovely way to get us both out of the house, have a joint hobby and get us moving. It's on our list of things to take up again and I'm really looking forward to it.

It doesn't have to be salsa if that's not your thing, but why not go to a group dance class with a friend, or even on your own? It's a brilliant way to meet new people while learning something new and getting your heart rate going at the same time. As a starting point, simply type 'Dance classes near me' into your search engine and go from there.

Journal Time ✍

Choose an activity from the previous pages that will get you moving in some way and isn't something you've done before – or at the very least is an activity you haven't tried for a while.

Alternatively, write down a few ideas of things you'd like to try, that will get you moving. Don't be intimidated by the list; write down anything that comes to mind. It doesn't have to be the usual stuff, why not go to Circus School and learn to master doing a handstand? (I bought vouchers for one near us for my husband's birthday and he now goes once a week and loves it!)

The only way that you'll move out of feeling afraid to try something new, or something you've given up, is to push yourself through it.

Work out what it is that you're really afraid of and remember that all you need is to be brave enough to suck at something new. It's the only way to ever get good at something! You may even enjoy it and make new friends, and if you don't, then just try something else. There's a *whole world* of new things out there just waiting for you to try them.

· ·

Your Get Moving! Challenge

· ·

As soon as you finish this chapter – which is in roughly 10 seconds' time – I want you to put on the You Just Need to Believe It Spotify playlist and start moving your body!

Enjoy this – you deserve it! Now is *your time to believe you can do it*.

· ·

DAY 10

Believe It!

*'Remember, you've been criticizing yourself
for years and it hasn't worked. Try approving
of yourself and see what happens.'*

LOUISE HAY

You did it! Isn't it amazing to think how far you've come in the past 10 days? Give yourself a pat on the back for sticking with this. It hasn't been easy. Some of it has been fun, some of it has been emotional, and some of it will have been hard. But you've stuck with it – and you should feel *so proud of yourself*.

♦ Have a look at those three things you wrote in your journal on Day 7, when you asked yourself what you'd attempt to do if you knew you couldn't fail. See how far you've come.

♦ How are you managing your daily rituals? Are they on their way to becoming part of your regular routine?

♦ When you're challenged, and this triggers your previously automatic fear response, are you ready with your new responses to bat it away? Which response has worked the best for you and why?

♦ Look back through your journal to see how your thought patterns have transformed over the past 10 days. Every step you've taken, no matter how small, is a step away from feeling stuck and scared, and you should feel *hugely* proud of yourself!

You made a promise to commit to investing in your beautiful self, and you did it. You *accept* that you're loved and that you're lovable; you accept that you're *worth* investing your time in, and that you're *capable* of incredible things.

Your Believe It! Challenge

You. Are. Incredible. And now it's time to start putting the things you've learned into practice.

Step 1

Commit to doing at least *one* of those three things you wrote in your journal on Day 7. *What would you attempt to do if you couldn't fail?* It doesn't have to be completed today, but you *do* have to start putting a *plan* in place to make that *one thing* happen.

Remember: *you just need to believe it* does *not* mean simply wishing things would get better or pretending that they're different to how they are. It means being prepared to look fear in the face and believe that you have it in you to tame it. It's having the self-belief and courage to keep going when things are tough, one step at a time.

And the more you do it, the smaller your fear becomes, because if you've overcome it once, you can do it again. And again. And again, and again, and again – and *that*, my beautiful friend, is the definition of unlocking your courage and reclaiming your power!

Step 2

Think of something in your life that you either do now, or have done in the past, that you thought was *impossible* to do or get. It can be anything at all. Perhaps it's the home you're living in now, which you barely notice any more – was there a time when you dreamed of living in a place like this?

Is it your relationship? The one that you take for granted because it's been part of your life for so long that you hardly think about it any more. Can you remember a time when you were alone and so wanted to have the companionship you now have? It can be anything: your healthy body, your friendship group, your children, your job – look around at your life until you find *one thing* that you used to long for and which you now have.

Journal Time ✍

Grab your journal and think about how it felt when the thing you wanted seemed really far away. How did you bring these things into your life? What did you face and overcome in order to get them? Write it all down in your journal.

There was a time in your life when you wanted something so much that you made it happen for you – it doesn't matter how small it is, you did it. You can do it again.

This one thing you want to do now, which seems so huge, so scary, is no bigger than the challenges you've faced before – these past 10 days have proven this to you. And if it seems that way, break it down into steps that take you, bit by bit, towards it.

Write it down. What's the first step you can take towards doing this one thing? It can be as simple as writing a list and then asking someone for help. Or Googling 'How to...' or 'Dance classes near me'. Now you have a plan.

Step 3

Schedule your plan to do that one thing. Author and coach Tony Robbins says, 'If you talk about it, it's a dream. If you envision it, it's possible. If you schedule it, it's real.' So, when are you going to commit time towards this plan?

If you wrote that you want to increase your fitness, schedule it in and be specific. Don't just write 'Do more exercise' – say what kind, for how long, where you're going to do it and who you'll do it with. If you wrote that you want to write a book, then schedule the time, write down how many words you want to produce each day and then sit down and do it! The words may not flow easily right away, but bit by bit you'll build up over time. Remember, excellence is what we consistently do, and you have the courage and self-belief to be excellent.

Now you're taking *action*! This is so important because you need to implant in your brain and your body that writing this list of things you're going to do and the action steps you're taking is *exciting not frightening*. Your body needs to *feel* how good it is to be doing this, and your brain needs to get caught up in the excitement.

This is a really important part of the process, so don't skip it! Because once your body and brain are excited about what you're doing, you're setting up brand-new triggers, so that every time you think of this one thing that you're going to do, you get excited. Your blood starts pumping and you feel energized just at the thought of it.

You have unlocked your courage.

. . . .

Congratulations!

I'm *so proud* of you! Ten days ago, you put out a post telling the world that you were dedicating this time to stepping away from the fear that's been holding you back. What are you going to tell your accountability buddies, who will be contacting you today to ask how you got on?

Take huge pride in telling the world how you feel. You deserve to shout it from the rooftops!

. . . .

You've done an incredible thing – so many people say that they want things to change, but they aren't brave enough to do anything about it.

. . . .

But you are – so shout about it! And let me know how you've got on! The fantastic thing about social media now is that you don't have to read this book on your own – you can tell me about your experience of doing the challenge! I *love* hearing from you. I genuinely feel like a proud big sister when I hear about what you've overcome by unlocking your fear and reclaiming your power!

I'd love for you to post a photo of yourself with this book and a caption sharing your experiences using #YouJustNeedToBelieveIt and tag me @andreamclean1 on Instagram or Andrea McLean on Facebook, so that I can see all the amazing progress you've made!

You can either put out the post below or make up one of your own:

'I've completed the You Just Need to Believe It: 10 Ways in 10 Days to Unlock Your Courage and Reclaim Your Power Challenge.'

Just make sure that underneath it you tell your story – what you were afraid of, what you overcame, and how incredible you feel today compared to just *10 days ago*. This is all about *you* and your incredible journey. Now you're capable of doing anything you set your mind to, with courage and conviction, because you now know that *you just need to believe it.*

To Infinity and Beyond

I t's *amazing* that you took this 10-day challenge, and you should now be feeling proud, fired up and ready to attempt the very things you were so afraid of! But this isn't the end of it. Now that you know what it is you need to do, you need to keep doing it.

What you've learned here isn't a quick fix – it's a kick-start to get you on the right track. Now you're on it, the important thing is to *stay* on it. That means maintaining your daily routines, remaining in a good headspace, and surrounding yourself with people who will lift and support you when you can feel yourself flagging.

To keep going on the path that you're on, the most important thing you need to do is be *consistent*. If you're going to carry on with the hard work that you've done on yourself over the past 10 days on your own, then I wish you all the very best – you've made huge strides in improving your attitude to fear and all the negative emotions and concerns that have been holding you back. Your life may never be the same again!

But, if you'd like to take this experience further, then I invite you to join my community of women who, like you, are committed to feeling excited about life's infinite possibilities and opportunities and are dedicated to supporting and encouraging each other and learning new ways to make this one life we're given a beautiful, interesting and inspiring experience.

When you become a member of this community, you'll be surrounded by women who feel the same way as you! You'll have access to *even more* incredible courses and challenges like the one you've just taken, along with masterclasses with experts to keep you informed and motivated, exclusive interviews with thought leaders to broaden your thinking and live community events led by me, during which you can interact with some of the world's leading life coaches and health and wellbeing experts.

Think of it as joining a gym for the mind where you'll learn to stay mentally strong. To find out more, visit www.thisgirlisonfire.com or look for the This Girl Is On Fire app on the App Store or Google Play.

Join us, and your life will never be the same again! Because that's what I'm here to do – change your life for the better. I've got your back. You're amazing. *You just need to believe it.*

References

Day 2

1. Cooley, C.H. (1902), *Human Nature and the Social Order*. New York: Charles Scribner's Sons

2. YouTube (2014), 'Jim Carrey at MIU: Commencement Address at the 2014 Graduation', youtube.com/watch?v=V80-gPkpH6M [Accessed November 2021]

3. YouTube (2020), 'Gareth Southgate still haunted by Euro 96 penalty miss as he opens up to Prince William', #SoundOfSupport, www.youtube.com/watch?v=jWXgUH44FZE [Accessed November 2021]

Day 4

1. YouTube (2014), 'University of Texas at Austin 2014 Commencement Address – Admiral William H. McRaven', www.youtube.com/watch?v=pxBQLFLei70 [Accessed November 2021]

2. Shetty, J. (2020), *Think Like a Monk: The Secret of How to Harness the Power of Positivity and Be Happy Now*. London: Thorsons

Day 8

1. Davies, Dr J. (2011), *The Importance of Suffering: The Value and Meaning of Emotional Discontent*. London: Routledge

2. Ibid.

Day 9

1. Pillay, Dr S. (2016), 'How simply moving benefits your mental health', https://www.health.harvard.edu/blog/how-simply-moving-benefits-your-mental-health-201603289350 [Accessed November 2021]

2. Mind, 'Physical activity and your mental health', www.mind.org.uk/information-support/tips-for-everyday-living/physical-activity-and-your-mental-health/about-physical-activity [Accessed November 2021]

Acknowledgements

This book started as an idea back in 2020, when I walked away from my career in TV after two decades to follow my heart. I was terrified, but also weirdly excited – 'nervouscited' as I like to call it. My announcement on live national TV led to a flurry of attention from the press and on social media. The focal point was something I said, based on the framed Erin Hansen poem I have hanging in my home: 'What if I fall?' 'Oh, but my darling, what if you fly?' I had said that I was afraid that I may fall, and I didn't know if that would happen or not, but I needed to know if I could fly...

Women of all ages contacted me in droves, saying that they, too, felt afraid, but they simply couldn't look their fear in the face, they just couldn't take that step away from the familiar and into the unknown... But they wanted to learn how.

So, I began to put together a structure, a collection of steps that I knew had worked for me to help me feel courage when I'd felt I had none, and had taught me how to love myself enough to believe that I deserved to live a life I love. This became the 10 Ways in 10 Days Challenge, which I served to my founding community. And I watched as they put their trust and faith in what I asked them to do, even when it was uncomfortable, and I cried with them when they emerged from the other side, euphoric with the transformations they'd experienced.

If it wasn't for these wonderful women, who have stayed with me on the bumpy journey that every new venture experiences and have continued to push through their fears and champion each other, this book wouldn't be in your hands right now. So to these women, I love all of you, and I'm eternally grateful for you.

To Nick. Yet again, you've believed in me, in us, and everything we are trying to achieve, and have given your love and support unwaveringly. You've understood when I've needed to lock myself away and lose myself in writing, hunched over my keyboard, headphones in and blocking out the world, leaving everyone to fend for themselves. Thank you for the endless supply of love, toast and coffee – my life fuel! I love you and I'm grateful for you.

To our children. I hope that you learn from the trials and errors of your parents and see that everything we do comes from a place of love and with a pure heart. May you always have courage.

To everyone at Hay House, thank you for believing not just in me but also in this book. Reid, Michelle, Jo, Emily, Lizzi, Tom, Debra, Helen, Julie, Diane, Katherine, Portia, Alexandra and Dan – you've all made this come to life and come to light and I'm so grateful for you. I love being part of your gang!

Nicky Johnston

About the Author

Andrea McLean was born in Scotland and grew up in Trinidad. After moving to England, she completed her education, backpacked around the world and then drove to London with everything she owned on the back seat of her car, sleeping on floors and working for free to pursue her dream of becoming a writer. Today she's the #1 *Sunday Times* bestselling author of *This Girl Is on Fire*, *Confessions of a Good Girl* and *Confessions of a Menopausal Woman*. She's also an award-winning broadcaster, journalist and the CEO/co-founder of the female personal growth site www.thisgirlisonfire.com

In her 26-year career as a broadcaster Andrea interviewed some of the biggest names in the business, including Oprah Winfrey, Beyoncé and Dustin Hoffman. For 13 years, she hosted ITV's multi-award-winning live national daytime chat show *Loose Women* with her signature warmth, humour and journalistic skill.

In 2020, Andrea left her TV role to pursue her passion for service and devote her time to empowering women through personal growth with her business, This Girl Is on Fire.

thisgirlisonfire.com

@OfficialTGIOF
@andreamclean1

Listen. Learn. Transform.

Listen to the audio version of this book for FREE!

Gain access to endless wisdom, inspiration, and encouragement from world-renowned authors and teachers—guiding and uplifting you as you go about your day. With the *Hay House Unlimited* Audio app, you can learn and grow in a way that fits your lifestyle . . . and your daily schedule.

With your membership, you can:

- Let go of old patterns, step into your purpose, live a more balanced life, and feel excited again.

- Explore thousands of audiobooks, meditations, immersive learning programs, podcasts, and more.

- Access exclusive audios you won't find anywhere else.

- Experience completely unlimited listening. No credits. No limits. No kidding.

Try for FREE!

HAY HOUSE

Look within

Join the conversation about latest products,
events, exclusive offers and more.

 Hay House

 @HayHouseUK

 @hayhouseuk

We'd love to hear from you!